COX'S GUIDE TO CHOOSING

RHODODENDRONS

COX'S GUIDE
RHODOD

TO CHOOSING ENDRONS

Peter & Kenneth Cox

Timber Press · Portland, Oregon

First published 1990

Typeset by Deltatype Ltd, Ellesmere Port, Cheshire and printed in Hong Kong for the publisher B. T. Batsford Ltd 4 Fitzhardinge St London W1H 0AH

First published in North America in 1990 by Timber Press, Inc. 9999 S.W Wilshire Portland, Oregan 97225

ISBN 0–88192–181–5

CONTENTS

LIST OF COLOUR PHOTOGRAPHS

LIST OF COLOUR PHOTOGRAPHS

INTRODUCTION

Those only familiar with the 'wild' rhododendron *ponticum* which has been receiving such bad press recently (deserved in most cases) would be surprised to learn that in fact there are over 800 different species of Rhododendron (including azaleas). These are found over a very large area of the world, from northern Australia, through Indonesia, south Asia, the Himalayas, Japan, Korea, Taiwan, into Europe and the Arctic, and also in north America. In addition to the species, there are over 10,000 named hybrids in existence throughout the world. With these statistics in mind, it can be seen that choosing rhododendrons is not always the easiest task. This book attempts to give a selection of the best of all the species and hybrids, chosen particularly for the diverse climactic conditions found in the UK. We do not include the very tricky malesian or vireya species from Indonesia and Malaya which are too tender to grow outdoors in Britain, but we give a wide survey of the best of the rest of this huge and varied genus. There are obvious omissions—we could not include everything—but from the 100+ species, 200 hybrids and our choice of both Japanese/evergreen azaleas and the deciduous kinds, it should be possible to select a large range of suitable plants for any UK garden—large or small, mild or cold. The omission of a species or hybrid from this book in no way means that it should not be grown. This book provides a guide to building a good representative collection, but newer, less well-known or rarer plants are also rewarding to grow, and are well worth searching for.

SPECIES OR HYBRIDS?

A very commonly asked question is whether to concentrate on species or hybrids. In our opinion, there is a simple answer: grow some of both. As a very over-generalized rule, species have more interesting foliage, but are less free-flowering and often harder to grow, requiring more favourable conditions. Hybrids are easier to grow, flower more freely and spectacularly, but have less interesting foliage. There are many exceptions to this, and we would always recommend a balance of species and hybrids in a collection for maximum impact and interest. The peak of species flowering is in April while the peak of hybrids is in May and early June; and a spread of flower from January to July and August should be possible with a mixture of species and hybrids in most UK gardens. As people become more and more interested in rhododendrons, they tend to move more and more towards species, often tearing up hybrids in disgust, leaving an imbalanced collection with a lack of really spectacular colour after April. Our collection at

Glendoick would be vastly diminished without either group, and we feel that species and hybrids are perfectly compatible. We make mixed plantings of dwarf species and hybrids, but generally keep larger species and hybrids in their own groups, but this is really a matter of personal choice.

Space does not permit us to give any but the briefest information on general cultivation of rhododendrons. More complete information on this can be found in many of the books outlined in the 'Further Information' section on p 167.

PLANTING AND CULTIVATION

As is well known, rhododendrons must have an acid soil i.e. between pH 4 and 6 for best results. In more alkaline areas, raised beds with peat can be used to grow the dwarfer kinds, and there are several species and hybrids which are somewhat tolerant of more alkaline conditions. Another option is to try to obtain plants grafted onto 'Cunningham's White' which imparts a degree of alkaline tolerance to plants normally needing a more acid soil. Rhododendrons like good drainage, but not dry conditions. Some of the hardy hybrids, most Japanese azaleas and many dwarfs thrive in full sun and in a fair amount of exposure, but many species and hybrids benefit from woodland conditions, in light (not dense) shade, with shelter from winds and frost. This does not require that you have a woodland, only that some shade and wind-shelter can be provided. The high walls and fences of urban gardens often provide these conditions ready made. The individual descriptions outline the favoured conditions of each plant.

Rhododendrons are fairly low-maintenance plants if they are in a site that suits them, and it is worth making a thorough preparation of their planting area. We recommend that an area considerably larger than the root size is dug over and that organic matter such as peat, bark, needles or leaf-mould are added to the soil. A combination of some or all of these is ideal. Rhododendrons are happiest in their own company, planted in groups, without competition from other greedy plants amongst their shallow roots. Dwarfs and evergreen azaleas are most successful planted *en masse*, in prepared beds, in groups of more than one of each variety if space permits. As the plants mature, they should form a dense mat, keeping weeds down and forming an easily maintained, undulating display of foliage and flowers. Deciduous azaleas too look best planted in bold groups so that the full range of colour contrasts can be appreciated. All this is not to say that you must have lots of room for rhododendrons. A small town garden can be filled with many of the dwarf and semi-dwarf types, giving a wide range of foliage and flower similar to that of the larger types. Even the smallest growers such as *keiskei* 'Yaku Fairy' and *keleticum* Radicans can become a superb feature in a smaller garden.

One of the best ways to keep rhododendrons in good health is to mulch them regularly. The best materials readily available are oak- and beech-leaf mould, conifer needles, composted conifer bark and shredded garden waste. Apply in late winter when the ground is wet. The mulch helps to retain moisture.

On a small or a large scale, informality is surely the key to the best effect. Create a landscape of diversity to fit into the space available. Straight lines and billiard-table lawns are not in keeping with the rounded, spreading, or upright shapes of rhododendrons. Make use of the diversity available, using striking colour combinations—yellow and purple, red and white, orange and lavender-blue—and try to plan for maximum length of flowering season, and the greatest use of foliage contrast. There are rhododendrons in flower almost every week of the year at Glendoick; there is no need to stick to the mid-season May-flowering types.

BUYING RHODODENDRONS

Rhododendrons are amongst the harder plants to produce commercially, in that they are slow to root from cuttings, and many species are virtually impossible. For this reason, commercially produced rhododendrons are produced by several different techniques, and it is well worth enquiring which method was used before buying, as all have particular advantages and drawbacks for the customer.

Cuttings

Most of the commonly available rhododendrons and azaleas sold in garden centres are raised from cuttings. These are taken in late summer and take 3–6 months to root. Cutting-grown plants are generally the most reliable and trouble-free, and most importantly, as this is a vegetative method, it reproduces the parent species or hybrid exactly. Unfortunately many rhododendrons are very hard or impossible to root, especially among the species, and other methods are used.

Seed

Of course the original source of every plant is seed. Whether of a species or hybrid, every seedling is unique, this can be both a blessing and a curse. Seedlings can show an enormous variation in quality of foliage, size and colour of flower, hardiness, disease-resistance, habit etc. Unless you can actually see the seedling in flower, and it can be proved to be hardy, disease-resistant etc., you may be left with a poor, if unique plant. Before making additional comments about species from seed, it should be made clear that NAMED hybrids should NEVER be bought as seedlings. Seedlings of a hybrid will not be identical to the parents; seedlings of a hybrid are NOT that hybrid and are usually inferior. That is not to say that hybrid seedlings are necessarily to be avoided at all costs. Many crosses between two species provide very uniform offspring, and we use this method of production for crosses made for foliage using *yakushimanum*, *pachysanthum*, *proteoides* and other species (see p 164).

Species from seed

There are two sources of species seed.

1. Seed from cultivated plants. With care, an excellent method of production, but rhododendrons easily hybridize with one another, and seed collected off open-pollinated (by insects) species will usually have been hybridized unless there are no other rhododendrons flowering at the same time. Do not buy species raised from seed unless they've been raised from hand-pollinated parents (deliberately pollinated). Even this is not a guarantee of true species, as many people do not pollinate carefully enough, or use incorrectly named parents. Some hard-to-propagate species are excellent from seed, and with continuous selection of the best parents, better and better seedlings can result. Two examples of this are our strains of pink *souliei* and red *camtschaticum*. Some very variable species are not good from hand-pollinated seed, as you are more than likely to be sold a poorer clone. The advantage of seed-raised species is that each plant is unique, making it worth planting a group to demonstrate variation, and there is a good chance that if the best forms of the parents have been used, fine new forms should result. In many cases seedlings make more compact plants than cutting-raised plants do. This is true of deciduous azaleas and of many species such as *bureavii*.

2. Wild seed. Seedlings from wild seed are quite commonly available, and in many ways these are the most exciting to grow, especially if the species are rare. One hopes that most collectors do correctly name what they collect, but this is not always the case. Sometimes wild seed contains natural hybrids, but the best nurseries ought to recognize these before they are sold. If you can get hold of wild seed e.g. from the rhododendron society seed exchanges, you can raise the seed yourself, which is a time-consuming if satisfying way to obtain new forms. Our own nursery and several others raise seedlings from expeditions to Asia and elsewhere. Collectors try to collect better forms of species, or hardier forms from higher elevations. The most exciting wild seed is that of rare or new species. Recently introduced ones include *kesangiae*, and *liliiflorum*. Such seedlings are usually the cheapest way to obtain rare and unusual plants. If you do grow wild seedlings, keep a note of the collector's number, preferably on the label and in a record book. These numbers e.g. *forrestii* Repens R. 59174 (referring to the collecting of Joseph Rock) are given to a species each time seed is collected in the wild and they give the plant a history which can be researched at any time in the future. The collector will usually have made field notes, and it is usually possible to find out exactly where the seed of that number was collected, at what altitude and on what date etc. The value of a species collection is greatly increased by the existence of collectors' numbers, and seedlings from the same number can be compared in other gardens. If space permits, it is well worth growing to flowering size a group of wild seedlings, from one number or one expedition (only 2–3 years from seed with some lepidotes, longer with most others) and selecting the best ones to keep as the plants mature. This need not take up a very large amount of room, as you can plant close together and thin out as soon as the flowers appear. Wild seed is a gamble, producing the most exciting and occasionally the most disappointing results, but overall it is one of the most satisfying ways to build a rhododendron collection.

Grafting

This method of propagation involves making a union between a rootstock which is already growing with a scion or shoot which has no roots. Many hard-to-root species and hybrids are produced this way, and the best clones of big-leaved species can usually only be produced by grafting. Grafted rhododendrons have a bad name in Britain because traditionally the 'wild' species *ponticum* was used as a rootstock. Although easy to graft on to, the rootstock is so vigorous, it usually sends up suckers which, if not removed, will eventually smother the species or hybrid grafted on top. Many old collections have been completely lost in this way. We do not recommend accepting plants grafted onto *ponticum* and if a nursery cannot tell you what rootstock was used, a grafted plant is probably better avoided. In Continental Europe, grafting is used for most larger hybrids, and they find that this produces hardier, more compact plants which often flower at a younger age than those from cuttings. If 'Cunningham's White' is used, (probably the best rootstock, and the most popular in West Germany) it passes on a tolerance of more alkaline conditions. Many other species and hybrids also make suitable rootstocks. Rootstocks other than *ponticum* can throw suckers when young which will come from, at or below the lump where the graft was made. These should be pulled or broken off at the stem rather than cut. If you want the best clones and forms of hard-to-root species such as the large-leaved ones and those from the Taliensia subsection, grafted plants are usually the only option, and in many cases easier-grown, freer-flowering plants will result compared to seed-raised plants.

Micro-propagation

Many plants are now propagated by this method which involves producing tiny plants in test-tubes with the help of hormones. These plantlets are rooted and slowly hardened off and grown on to saleable size. At present, it is mostly the more popular hybrids that are raised this way, plus new introductions. As a result a large number of plants becomes available much more quickly than by the conventional cutting or grafting methods of propagating. While in the long run this will lead to a plentiful supply of probably cheaper plants, there are dangers too. New hybrids that have not proved their worth may be produced in huge quantities and distributed before their drawbacks are discovered. Plantlets that have been incorrectly treated with the chemicals used in their production are often very slow to show typical characteristics, and occasionally horrible distorted plants result. Many naming mix-ups have occurred. These problems are all something which a good nursery should be aware of. At best, this method can produce more compact and vigorous plants than conventional means, and if a plant produced in this way looks healthy, then it is probably going to grow very well.

Layering

This is still the best method of vegetative propagation for the amateur who has no propagating facilities. Branches near the ground are pushed and anchored to the soil, and should form roots. Some nurseries use this method for hard-to-root species and hybrids, but the resulting plants can be of a rather poor shape, as the lowest part of the stem has been horizontal. We find layering best for hard-to-root lepidotes which can be easily pruned later into an acceptable shape.

All the above propagation methods can produce fine healthy plants and, equally, poor and straggly, sickly ones. Visit the nursery you buy from if you can, as there is no better substitute than seeing the plants growing. A weed-covered, untidy nursery will usually produce poor plants. One of the largest problems with buying rhododendrons is being sure of correctly labelled plants. It is a lifetime's work to be able to identify rhododendrons well, and small plants are hard to recognize. Even the best nurseries sometimes sell 'so-called' species from contaminated seed, and if you are looking for rare or unusual plants it is well worth researching what you expect the plant to look like, so you can spot errors. There are only a few rhododendron nurseries which do sell the best correctly labelled plants, and if you want other than the hybrids commonly found in most garden-centres, it is worth buying from specialists (see p. 168). Advice can usually be obtained from the rhododendron societies (see p. 167).

HOW TO USE THIS BOOK

Rhododendron species, hybrids, deciduous azaleas and evergreen azaleas are all given separate alphabetical listings. Under the one heading, other similar species or hybrids can be found. For example under *cinnabarinum* all the subspecies and varieties can be found, as well as the related species *keysii*. Under the hybrid 'Golden Torch' heading several other lower-growing yellow hybrids can be found. This method saves space and allows easy comparison between similar plants. Within each entry, species and hybrids are cross-referenced. This is indicated by capital letters. We have also included lists of rhododendrons and azaleas (p. 164) according to features such as flower colour, foliage characteristics and hardiness. We have tried to avoid too many scientific or botanical terms which tend to make indigestible reading. Essential terms are contained in the glossary on p. 166. The following notes accompany the key on p. 16.

Climate

Each species or hybrid has been assigned a hardiness rating which should indicate its suitability for different areas. The United States Department of Agriculture (USDA) hardiness rating is also given.

H5 (USDA 5–6a) −5° to −10° F (−21° to −23° C). Hardy anywhere in the British Isles, although wind shelter may be necessary.

H4 (USDA 6b) 0° F (−18° C). Should be hardy in all but the severest climates inland or at high altitude. Wind shelter is advisable, and some species and hybrids may grow or flower early or late, requiring extra care.

H3 (USDA 7a) +5° F (−15° C). Suitable for southern and western gardens, and in favourable sites elsewhere. Find a site with good frost drainage and shelter from wind. In colder districts, severe winters may cause damage, but most will recover.

H2 (USDA 7b–8a) +10° F (−12° C). For sheltered gardens in west, and in southern Ireland. Well worth trying in colder gardens in the most favourable sites but liable to be killed in severest winters without extra artificial protection. Otherwise greenhouse cultivation.

H1 (USDA 8b) +15° F to +20° F (−10° C to −8° C). Western islands in favourable sites, and greenhouse cultivation elsewhere.

These ratings are little more than a relative guide. Microclimates allow tender rhododendrons to be grown in more northern and eastern areas, and within one small garden some sites can be far less cold than others. Using partially shaded south-facing walls, sheltered banks, and/or occasional cloche or other protection, tender or tricky species and hybrids can be grown in severer gardens. At Glendoick, where our minimum temperature is 0° F (−

18° C), we grow some H2 (USDA 7b/8a) species and hybrids successfully in favourable sites, and they only suffer in our severest winters. Take some risks with your plantings; the severest winters only occur from time to time, and tender plants can give many years of pleasure.

Height and Size

Again, the sizes given are only a guide. Some rhododendrons have a tall column-like habit, some grow as wide as high, and others tend towards a spreading habit. Grow a mixture of these for the most interesting effects. The figure given below refers to approximate height in 10 years, although this varies greatly, with more shaded, moist and western sites providing much longer yearly growth than sunny, dry or colder ones. Many of the dwarfer types grow wider than high, and these are mentioned in the text.

Dwarf	to 40 cm/1½ft
Semi-dwarf	40–80cm/1½–3ft
Low	80–135cm/3–4½ft
Medium	135–180cm/4½–6ft
Tall	180cm+/6ft+

Awards

These have been given to rhododendrons in the UK, USA and elsewhere. They are a reasonable guide to quality, but many good species and hybrids have not received awards, so don't place too much reliance on them. Award forms of species are usually fine clones well worth seeking out, although an F.C.C. clone of a species does not necessarily mean that it is the very best available, as new forms are constantly appearing. With many older hybrids, a whole grex or group of seedlings was released under one name, e.g. 'FABIA', 'LADY CHAMBERLAIN' etc., and named and award clones e.g. 'FABIA A.M.', 'FABIA TANGERINE', 'LADY CHAMBERLAIN F.C.C.' should be sought.

UK awards in ascending order of merit (awards with a 'T' were awarded after trials at Wisley Gardens, Surrey):

F.C.C.(T)=first class certificate (the highest award)
A.M.(T)=award of merit
H.C.(T)=highly commended

USA awards in ascending order of merit:

S.P.A.=superior plant award (the highest accolade, rarely awarded)
A.E.=award of excellence
C.A.=conditional award

Gold and silver medals are awarded in Holland, Belgium and West Germany.

KEY

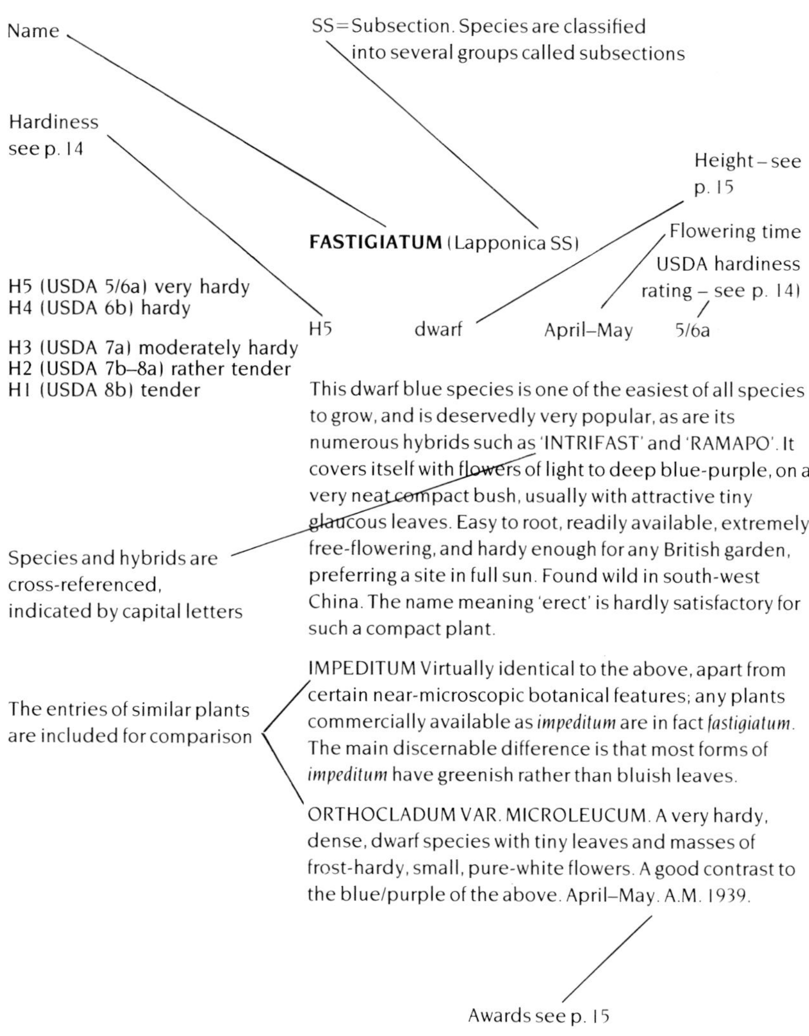
Name
SS=Subsection. Species are classified into several groups called subsections
Hardiness see p. 14
Height – see p. 15
Flowering time
USDA hardiness rating – see p. 14)
FASTIGIATUM (Lapponica SS)
H5 (USDA 5/6a) very hardy
H4 (USDA 6b) hardy
H3 (USDA 7a) moderately hardy
H2 (USDA 7b–8a) rather tender
H1 (USDA 8b) tender
H5
dwarf
April–May
5/6a
This dwarf blue species is one of the easiest of all species to grow, and is deservedly very popular, as are its numerous hybrids such as 'INTRIFAST' and 'RAMAPO'. It covers itself with flowers of light to deep blue-purple, on a very neat compact bush, usually with attractive tiny glaucous leaves. Easy to root, readily available, extremely free-flowering, and hardy enough for any British garden, preferring a site in full sun. Found wild in south-west China. The name meaning 'erect' is hardly satisfactory for such a compact plant.
Species and hybrids are cross-referenced, indicated by capital letters
IMPEDITUM Virtually identical to the above, apart from certain near-microscopic botanical features; any plants commercially available as *impeditum* are in fact *fastigiatum*. The main discernable difference is that most forms of *impeditum* have greenish rather than bluish leaves.
The entries of similar plants are included for comparison
ORTHOCLADUM VAR. MICROLEUCUM. A very hardy, dense, dwarf species with tiny leaves and masses of frost-hardy, small, pure-white flowers. A good contrast to the blue/purple of the above. April–May. A.M. 1939.
Awards see p. 15

ALPHABETICAL LISTINGS

SPECIES

ABERCONWAYI (Irrorata SS)

H4 low-medium May–June 6b

Named after the late Lord Aberconway from Bodnant in Wales who financed the first collecting of this species from Yunnan Province, China. This medium-sized rhododendron is grown mainly for its unusual flat, saucer-shaped flowers, borne in trusses of 6–12. These are white, tinged pink, and are usually prominently spotted with crimson. Its leaves are also unusual, being thick, rigid and brittle, with sharp points at the end. It has a tendency to become sparse and straggly, but some pinching and pruning and a reasonably open site usually ensures a reasonable shape. Hardy enough for almost all of the UK, and flowering in late May and early June, it avoids most spring frosts. Fair to root from cuttings and flowering from 4–5 years old. Selected forms should be sought, as the flowers of seedlings of this variable species may be disappointing. The clone usually commercially available is '**His Lordship**' A.M. 1945.

ADENOGYNUM (Taliensia SS)

H5 low-medium March–May 6a

Species of the Taliensia subsection were somewhat despised until fairly recently, largely because of their slowness to bloom. Now there are many Taliensia fanatics who seek them out in preference to all other species. This group consists of hardy, long-lived, generally easily grown plants; most have good to excellent foliage, with an attractive indumentum on the leaf underside. The flowers do usually take some years to appear but are then usually freely produced in small, neat trusses, in shades of pink or white, often spotted or blotched. R. *adenogynum* is typical of the subsection in flower with leathery leaves with a dense woolly indumentum below. The habit is usually compact and flat-topped. It grows wild in the mountains of western China, above and just below the tree line, where it is plentiful. New forms have recently been introduced. Not easy to root and takes some years to bloom, but hardy in all of the UK and quite easy to cultivate in good soil conditions. Many related species such as ***R. aganniphum***, ***balfourianum***, ***phaeochrysum***, ***przewalskii*** and ***traillianum*** are also well worth growing, as should be the new introduction ***R. bhutanense***.

phaeochrysum var. *levistratum*

ARBOREUM (Arborea SS)

H2–4 tall March–May 7b/8a–6b

One of the most variable of all species, in flower and hardiness, and also in foliage. Flowers, in compact trusses, vary from deep red through pink to white. The blood-red forms which come from low elevations in the wild are the most tender, while most pink and white higher-elevation forms will grow in sheltered gardens. Its name suggests its tree-like habit, and grand specimens—some over 100 years old—can be seen in many old west-coast gardens with massive, rough trunks. Even if cut back by severest winters, it can often regenerate from old trunks. Leaves are usually thick and leathery, deep green above with white, silvery or brown indumentum below. One of the first species to be introduced into cultivation from S.E. Asia and much used in

arboreum ssp. *delavayi*

the parentage of early 19th-century hybrids by the Waterer family and others. It is found in the wild over a wide area: **ssp. *arboreum*** and ***cinnamomeum*** from the Himalayas, ***delavayi*** from western China and Burma and ***zelanicum*** from Sri Lanka. Subspecies ***cinnamomeum*** is the hardiest and the only one to have flowers giving the full variation of red through pink to white. Its leaves have dark rusty brown to fawn indumentum below. All the others have flowers of shades of red or occasionally pink. R. *arboreum* is very common in many areas of the Himalayan foothills and it is the species that most people see when trekking there, forming trees up to 100ft high, presenting a magnificent sight in full flower. Easily grown under woodland conditions, it takes several years to start blooming. Special forms are usually grafted but there are many new introductions coming from wild seed most years.

AUGUSTINII (Triflora SS)

H3–4 medium April–May 7a–6b

One of the best-loved species for moderate gardens, this is the bluest of the larger lepidote species. Unfortunately, the bluest selections tend to be the most tender while those with paler flowers are hardier. Smallish, rather narrow leaves on a bush of stiff erect habit. Named after Augustine Henry, an Irish medical officer in China. Common in central-west China where it was collected mostly by E. H. Wilson. Often has purplish to pink flowers in the wild, the cultivated clones being mostly garden selections. Quite easy to root and flowers from about 3–5 years old. The hardier selections are suitable for most UK gardens with a little shelter. No special requirements except some protection for the rather early young growth on young plants. There are numerous selections from Tower Court, Bodnant, Exbury etc. and we also recommend the excellent '**Electra**', with large blue flowers. This is a cross between **ssp. *augustinii*** and **ssp. *chasmanthum***. The latter comes from further west into Yunnan with lavender-blue flowers in more compact trusses. R. *augustinii* is one of the parents of numerous dwarf and medium-sized blue-purple hybrids such as 'BLUE TIT', 'BLUE DIAMOND', 'ST BREWARD' etc. Most of these are hardier and are more suitable for smaller, windier or colder gardens. Readily available.

CONCINNUM. One of the hardiest of the Triflorums and a better alternative to *augustinii* in coldest areas. Flowers of various shades of pinkish lavender to reddish purple. The best selections have the latter colour which is quite striking. The smallish leaves are usually quite dark on a reasonably compact plant. Wild in west central and central China where it is common. Easily rooted and blooms fairly young. The clone usually offered, which has deep ruby-red flowers, was raised at Tower Court; others are occasionally available. Hardy throughout the UK and easy to grow in open woodland.

AMBIGUUM is similar but with yellow flowers.

AURICULATUM (Auriculata SS)

H4 tall July–August 6b

One of the latest of all species to flower, it has large loose trusses of scented, white or pale-pink flowers, blotched green in the centre. Long pointed leaves, often rather pale in colour. Grows into a large vase-shaped specimen under good conditions. Wild in west central China. Usually propagated from hand-pollinated seed or grafted, and fairly readily available. Takes some years to start blooming. While it is hardy, its growth comes very late, so it is unsuitable for cold or/and high elevation gardens where the growth can be damaged by early frosts. Needs shelter and the roots must be kept moist when in growth. Inclined to look unhealthy with sparse foliage but very fine when well-grown. A parent of several late-flowering hybrids such as 'POLAR BEAR' and 'LODAURIC' which are easier to grow in colder gardens and which are more successful at Glendoick.

BARBATUM (Barbata SS)

H3–4 medium-tall February–April 7a–6b

One of the early-flowering red species, and therefore seen at its best in milder and western gardens. Very compact trusses of the brightest scarlet flowers. Fairly long, pointed, generally dark-green leaves, usually with bristles on the leaf stalks, hence its name. Has a lovely flaking purplish bark. Forms a fine large rounded bush when well-grown. Common in the western and central Himalayas. Not for severest climates, either for its hardiness or its early flowers which are often frosted but well worth-growing in sheltered woodland in colder areas. There have been several new introductions in recent years but these often do not compare well with earlier importations. Not easy to root or graft so perhaps best-grown from wild or hand-pollinated seed. Quite readily available.

ARGIPEPLUM, closely related, has more rounded leaves, brilliant copper-plum coloured when young and smaller flowers.

BUREAVII (Taliensia SS)

H4–5 low-medium April–May 6b–6a

This species has foliage amongst the finest of all rhododendrons, and is therefore very popular. A thick reddy-brown, woolly indumentum covers the leaf undersides and the stems, and remains attractive all the year round. On the young leaves, the indumentum is more of a silvery pink colour, providing a fine contrast with the rufous colouring of the older ones. The flowers are attractive but sometimes rather unspectacular, pale pink to white and usually spotted with crimson and purple in

barbatum

bureavii 'Ardrishaig' A.M.

loose trusses of 10–20. Although hardy enough for almost anywhere in the UK, it needs a fair amount of shelter from wind to keep its fine foliage in good condition. Fairly hard to root, and rather thick-stemmed for grafting, we find it easiest to raise from hand-pollinated seed; the seedlings show their fine foliage from 2–3 years of age. Although it takes a number of years to start flowering, the foliage of *bureavii* is so fine, that it is a must for any collection. **'Ardrishaig'** A.M. 1988 has the finest flowers, but not the best foliage.

ELEGANTULUM is a similar species with a less dense habit and longer, narrower leaves with fine indumentum below, pinkish when young, turning to brown. The flowers, produced at a younger age, are shades of pale pink with small crimson spots. Easy, reliable and should be more widely grown.

RUFUM is another related species with indumentum rivalling *bureavii*. Flowers white to pink. Very hardy, but a little early into growth.

CALOPHYTUM (Fortunea SS)

H5 tall February–April 6a

This is the largest-leaved species hardy enough for any UK garden. The large flowers are in fine trusses of white to pink, blotched or spotted crimson. The long, narrow, pointed leaves cover a very large, wide-growing plant which needs plenty of room and makes a long-lived umbrella-shaped specimen. Grows wild in the mountains of western Sichuan, China where it is common. Original introductions were by Wilson, but it has been re-introduced recently from Emei Shan. Needs to be grafted or grown from wild or hand-pollinated seed. Slow to bloom and like other big-leaved species, it does not bloom every year. Quite readily commercially available. Well worth growing for its foliage, and while very hardy, the large leaves require shelter from wind. Usually easy to grow but may prefer drier or more eastern areas.

calophytum ➤

calostrotum 'Gigha' F.C.C.

SUTCHUENENSE is closely related, with slightly shorter, less handsome leaves than the above. The flowers, of various shades of pink, with or without a blotch, are produced at a younger age than those of *calophytum*. Equally hardy and has a similar flowering time.

CALOSTROTUM (Saluenensia SS)

H4–5 dwarf-low May 6b–6a

A first-rate dwarf, especially in the clone **'Gigha'**. Large flat-faced flowers, usually shades of rich purple, very freely produced on an attractive plant with silvery foliage, hence the name which means 'with a beautiful covering'. Habit usually compact. In the wild it grows high on the moorlands of north Burma and south-west China where it forms carpets. Cuttings are fairly easily rooted and it flowers as a very young plant. Readily available. Easily grown in an open situation and an excellent subject for near or at the front of a bed of dwarfs. **'Gigha'** F.C.C., very compact with masses of large, rose-crimson flowers, is one of the best of all dwarfs. There are numerous other forms and the following less widely available ones are also well worth growing: **ssp. *riparioides*** Rock's form is taller-growing with large, deep-purple flowers, often opening in autumn in addition to spring, and deep bluish-green leaves. **Ssp. *riparium* Calciphilum** has smaller leaves and delicate pink flowers in late May. **Ssp. *riparium* Nitens** lacks the silvery foliage but has fine pinkish-purple flowers in June–July, one of the latest-flowering of all dwarfs.

◄ *sutchuenense*

CAMPANULATUM (Campanulata SS)

H4 medium-tall March–May 6b

One of the most widespread and common Himalayan species and often seen in some quantity in older British woodland gardens. This is very variable in flower and foliage, some being much superior to others, but the best flowers are often not on the best foliage plants. Flowers many shades of lavender, purple, near-blue, to pure white, spotted to a variable degree, in compact-to-loose trusses. The variable leaves can be very attractive when young, especially those with a bluish tinge. Habit bushy to occasionally tree-like with age and the indumentum on the underside varies from light fawn to a rich rusty brown. Starts to flower once it reaches 4–5ft. Has been re-introduced many times in recent years from Nepal with the largest-leaved western forms being the most desirable. Most introductions are hardy enough for the majority of fairly sheltered gardens where it is easy to grow. Very hard to root, but it is worth searching out grafted plants of selected clones. '**Knaphill**' has good foliage and the nearest to blue flowers. '**Roland Cooper**' A.M. has very large leaves and good flowers.

Ssp. AERUGINOSUM has a low, compact habit and often undistinguished magenta flowers. In its best forms it has magnificent bluish young growth, amongst the finest in the genus, and is mainly grown as a foliage plant.

WALLICHII differs only in having a scattered-to-absent indumentum and is essentially an eastern form of *campanulatum*. Usually less impressive as a foliage plant.

campanulatum 'Roland Cooper' A.M.

campylocarpum

CAMPYLOCARPUM
(Campylocarpa SS)

H3–4 low-medium April–May 7a–6b

One of the most versatile and easiest to grow of the yellow species, it has been much used in hybridizing, to produce 'UNIQUE', 'CARITA', 'MOONSTONE' and many others. Found over a wide area of the western Himalayan region, it is quite variable. Flowers are bell-shaped, in loose trusses of 6–10, pale to bright yellow, occasionally pink to white, sometimes blotched red. Smooth leaves are rounded at the end, and the plant is generally fairly dense and compact. The hardiest forms should be suitable for most British gardens in a sheltered position, but avoid too much shade, as this tends to cause straggly, shy-flowering specimens. Forms sold as var. 'elatum' are usually taller and less dense growing, and sometimes have orange tips to the flowers. There do not seem to be any outstanding award forms in the trade in the UK, but we recommend the more compact forms with clear-yellow flowers. Widely available. **Ssp. caloxanthum** is a more dwarf form of the above species, with a very attractive, dense mounding habit. The best forms also have striking glaucous-blue foliage. Creamy-yellow to sulphur-yellow, bell-shaped flowers often opening from orange buds. It demands excellent drainage to prevent a tendency for the stem to rot. It is worth extra care and a good site, as it is very free-flowering and has an excellent habit and foliage. Widely available.

campylogynum SBEC

CALLIMORPHUM, although classed as a different species, is really just an eastern, pink-flowered variant of the above subspecies. Pink to deep-rose-pink flowers, usually with a deeper blotch, in loose trusses of 4–8, appear from late April to early June, depending on the form. Similar in appearance and likes conditions similar to those for *caloxanthum*. Widely available.

CAMPYLOGYNUM (Campylogyna SS)

H3–4 dwarf-semi-dwarf April/May 7a–6b

One of the most varied and best of all dwarf species, it is worth making a collection of different forms if you have room. We have over 10 distinct ones, and there are many more. All have thimble-shaped flowers on the ends of stalks, carrying them above the foliage. The colours available include purple through to red, pink and white, and they vary in height from 2in to 4ft (5 cm to 1.2 m). Those with claret and other dark-coloured flowers have dense dark shiny leaves, making neat foliage plants when out of flower. The paler-flowered forms generally have paler leaves. All form compact plants though some are more upright in habit than others. Found wild from the eastern Himalayas to Yunnan, usually above the tree-line. Most are fairly easily rooted and free-flowering from a young age. Variable in hardiness, the majority of forms being suitable for most UK gardens but all resent too much hot sun and dry roots. There are several forms and clones, some of which were formerly recognized as species. **Leucanthum** A.M. has creamy white flowers; not very vigorous. **Celsum** is the tallest form. **Charopoeum** has the biggest leaves and flowers—the clone **'Patricia'** is perhaps the easiest *campylogynum* to please; flowers plum.

Cremastum has leaves with green undersides, in contrast to all the others which are silvery beneath; flowers variable; **'Bodnant Red'** A.M. has red flowers. **Myrtilloides** is the lowest-growing with the smallest flowers, variable in flower colour and hardiness—one clone of Farrer 1046 has near-black flowers and the darkest shiny leaves, but is rather tender.

CAMTSCHATICUM (subgenus *Therorhodion*)

H5 dwarf May–June and often into autumn 5/6a

A most unusual and distinctive deciduous dwarf, considered by some not to be a rhododendron at all. The almost flat flowers, on long stalks, are usually shades of purple but there are now red, pink and white forms cultivated. The hairy leaves cover a creeping, suckering little shrub, rarely more than a few inches high. The name signifies that it comes from Kamtchatka in eastern Siberia but its distribution stretches from northern Japan up to and across the Bering Straits into Alaska. Quite easily propagated from soft cuttings, seed or sometimes division. We have flowered it in one year from seed. The red, pink and white forms are still rare but these often come true from seed if isolated. Not often available in southern England where it is hard to grow, preferring cooler summers further north, and very common in parts of northern Europe. Best grown in full sun with a moist root run. Very hardy but the young growth is susceptible to spring frosts.

CERASINUM (Thomsonia SS)

H4 medium May–June 6b

An unusual Himalayan species which always attracts comment. There are two flower variations, both in loose trusses of 3–5. The most popular type is a bicolor, creamy/pink with a deeper-red rim round the edge of the flower. This is generally known as **'Cherry Brandy'**. The other less common type has scarlet flowers and is known as **'Coals of Fire'**. A neat, fairly compact species which can be rather shy-flowering, but is generally hardy and quite easy to please. Useful for its late flowering. Availability limited.

cerasinum

ciliatum

ECLECTEUM A related species whose name suggests its eclectic nature—its flowers can be virtually any colour, from white to purple, red, pink, yellow or a combination of these. Some forms are very poor and muddy, so selected ones should be sought out. A medium-sized bush flowering in March–April, earlier in some forms. Susceptible to powdery mildew. Availability limited.

VISCIDIFOLIUM Another related species which is one of the few to have orange flowers. Coppery-red to coppery-orange waxy flowers in loose trusses, opening in May. Susceptible to powdery mildew. Availability limited.

CILIATUM (Maddenia SS)

H3(–4) low March–May 7a(–6b)

One of the hardiest and dwarfest members of the Maddenia subsection. Very freely-produced white flushed pink, or white, flowers and quite attractive hairy foliage and peeling bark. Compact when young but leggy with age in shade. It is a native of the Himalayas where it was first found by Joseph Hooker in 1849 but it has been re-collected in recent years. Easily rooted, flowers from a young age and fairly readily obtainable. Not for gardens colder than Glendoick, where it is occasionally severely damaged, but it is always worth replacing. Some forms bloom as early as late February and are easily frosted. **B.L.M. 324** is a good introduction.

LEUCASPIS H2–3 (7b/8a–7a) Another early-flowering, rather tender species. Beautiful, flat, white flowers with contrasting black anthers in March. Hairy leaves. Best in western districts, although we can just keep it alive outside at Glendoick.

CINNABARINUM (Cinnabarina SS)

H3–4 medium-tall April–June 7a–6b

A most unusual and extremely variable species. Formerly divided into different species and varieties, it is now split into three subspecies. All have waxy, tubular, pendant or semi-pendant flowers in many colours and combinations of colours. Some have beautiful bluish-grey young foliage. The habit is usually upright and open but a few are compact. Found wild from the central Himalayas to Burma, where it grows around the tree-line. First introduced by Joseph Hooker from Sikkim in 1849. As it is so variable, it is important to propagate selected clones which are usually quite easily rooted. Several selections are generally available. Most forms are hardy enough for all but the coldest parts of the UK but are subject to bark-split from spring frosts. Quite easy to cultivate but unfortunately very susceptible to powdery mildew, especially in its numerous hybrids with *MADDENII* blood such as 'LADY CHAMBERLAIN'.

Ssp. *cinnabarinum* usually has various shades of orange flowers.
Blandfordiiflorum usually has bi- or tricolour flowers, in mixtures of red, orange and yellow, often late-flowering and amongst the hardiest;
A. M. Bodnant form is a good one.
Roylei has plum-crimson flowers with a bloom, young foliage often bluish: one of the best.
Ssp. *xanthocodon* has pale-yellow to yellow flowers, smaller than the above with lighter-coloured leaves.
Concatenans has beautiful near-orange flowers; leaves very attractive bluish-grey on a compact bush. ***Purpurellum*** has flowers in shades of purple with rather smaller leaves, A.M. clone being the best. Seems to be resistant to mildew.
Ssp. *tamaense* has flowers in shades of purple to lavender; leaves almost deciduous.
Ssp. *Xanthocodon* and **Purpurellum** resistant to mildew, **Roylei** moderately resistant.

cinnabarinum ssp. *xanthocodon*

cinnabarinum Roylei

dauricum 'Hokkaido' A.M.

KEYSII is a closely related species with clusters of tubular flowers which are usually bicolour red with yellow tips, but are sometimes all red. (Unicolor group.) Recently reintroduced from Bhutan.

DAURICUM (Rhodorastra SS)

H5 semi dwarf-medium December–April 5

One of the hardiest of all rhododendrons, found wild from the Russian Steppes to Siberia and in Northern China, Korea and Japan, it can sail unscathed through the worst British weather with ease! Flowers range from pale to deep rosy purple, and selected forms exist in shades of pink and white. Most forms of this species are deciduous or semi-deciduous, the flowers appearing on the ends of the nearly bare stems. Forms holding onto their leaves usually turn a copper or purple colour during the autumn and winter. Very useful for its extreme hardiness and early flowering, it has passed both traits on to its well-known progeny such as the hybrids 'PJM' and 'PRAECOX'. Free-flowering from an early age. The following two are among the best forms. **'Midwinter'** F.C.C. 1969 is one of the first of all species to bloom, often opening in December, and with bright rose-purple flowers able to withstand some frost—a reliable performer, providing a good contrast with ***Hamamelis*** and ***Jasminium nudiflorum***. **'Hokkaido'** A.M. 1979 has large white flowers; later-flowering than the above, usually March–April. Other good clones are also available.

mucronulatum var. *chejuense*

MUCRONULATUM A similar, equally hardy species, usually fully deciduous. Free-flowering with longer pointed leaves. Flowers rosy-purple, through rose-pink to white, opening from January to April. Many clones exist, one of the best being **'Cornell Pink'**, a pink selection from the USA. We also recommend the white forms, and the dwarf selections (**var. *chejuense***) from Cheju island in Korea. The latter do not bloom until March–April and have excellent autumn colour.

decorum

DECORUM (Fortunea SS)

H3–4 medium-tall late
April–July 7a–6b

A superb versatile species, tough enough in its hardiest forms for almost all British gardens. Found in south-west China and Burma, and many new introductions have been made in recent years. Found in a wide altitudinal range,it is important to seek out hardier forms from higher elevations. Some low-altitude collections have been damaged or killed at Glendoick, while the hardiest introductions thrive here in exposed situations in full sun. Fragrant flowers range from pale rose to white, some with spotting and markings of green or red, in usually open-topped trusses of 7–14. Leaves are oblong, smooth and medium-green, sometimes bronzy when young, on a very vigorous plant which usually begins to flower from a young age. This species is tolerant of slightly alkaline soils, and will also grow in drier growing situations than most other species, so able to extend the rhododendron garden to areas thought unsuitable for them. Easily raised from hand-pollinated seed off selected forms, from which both pink and white seedlings can be produced.

HEMSLEYANUM One of the many related species in the Fortunea subsection, this is a open tree-forming plant with scented flowers, white or pink-tinged, w a greenish yellow throat. This species is especially valuable for its unusual large crinkly edged leaves and its July–August flowering. Needs a sheltered site to protect its buds and large foliage, but otherwise hardy enough for most of Britain.

dichroanthum ssp. *scyphocalyx*

DICHROANTHUM (Neriiflora SS)

H4 low May–June 6b

One of the few orange species, and so very useful for extending the colour range of a collection. This species in its various forms is the background to most of the orange hybrids available, including 'FABIA', 'SONATA', 'GOLDSWORTH ORANGE' and many others. Thick, waxy, tubular, bell-shaped flowers in loose trusses, of various shades of red, orange, salmon, pink and yellow, often a combination of colours; many forms are a decidedly muddy mixture, and are not to everyone's taste. The name actually means 'with flowers of two colours'. The plant is dense and compact, and leaves have silvery indumentum below. Usually hardy, although somewhat vulnerable to late spring frosts. Found wild in west Yunnan, and recently re-introduced. Fairly easy to root and quite readily available. Requires good drainage and grows well in an open site in milder, wetter areas. A good form is **Forrest 6781**. **Ssp. *apodectum*** has slightly smaller, more shiny leaves with usually thicker indumentum. **Ssp. *scyphocalyx*** has less shiny leaves and thinner indumentum.

edgeworthii

EDGEWORTHII (Edgeworthia SS) including *bullatum*

H2–3 low-medium April–May 7b/8a–7a

A plant worth a great deal of trouble to satisfy its rather special needs. Large, sweetly scented white or white-flushed-pink flowers, usually in trusses of 3. The leaves have a distinctive, rough, grooved upper surface and rust-to-fawn-coloured woolly indumentum below. Habit compact to leggy. Named for a Mr Edgeworth of the Bengal Civil Service by Joseph Hooker who discovered it in Sikkim in 1849, and it is also found as far east as Yunnan. In the wild, this species is often epiphytic (grows on another plant—a tree-trunk for instance) or is found on rocks and cliffs and this indicates its requirement of good drainage. It will only grow well in very sandy soil, in a raised bed or on rocks or tree stumps in plenty of organic matter. Fairly easy to root or may be grown from hand-pollinated seed. Some forms are much hardier than others and these hardier forms may be grown successfully in the more favoured sites away from the western seaboard, even in eastern Scotland. Most forms are free-flowering from a young age. Quite readily available. One of the parents of many of the tender scented hybrids such as 'FRAGRANTISSIMUM' and 'LADY ALICE FITZWILLIAM'.

FACETUM (Parishia SS)

H2–3 medium-tall June–August 7b/8a–7a

It is a pity that such a fine red-flowered species is suitable only for the milder southern and western woodland gardens. Compact trusses of bright-red flowers, late in the season. A compact-to-leggy plant, with quite large leaves with a loose, light brown indumentum below. Native in the forests of the Burma-Yunnan border from where it has been recently re-introduced. Moderate to root and blooms quite young for such a large grower. Not widely available commercially on account of its tenderness. Shelter and moisture are needed for its late growth. Sometimes still grown under its old name *eriogynum*. This species and its close relative ***elliottii*** have been much used in hybridizing to raise fine red hybrids such as 'TALLY HO' and 'KILIMANJARO'.

FALCONERI (Falconera SS)

H3(–4) tall late April–June 7a (–6b)

This majestic species has the special merit of having the longest-lasting flowers of all rhododendrons, often for a month or more. Large full trusses of heavily textured creamy-white to pale-yellow flowers with a dark blotch. Magnificent large leaves, up to 12 in (30.5 cm) long, rough above and with rusty indumentum below. It eventually grows into a broad-crowned small tree with an attractive red-brown bark. Takes some years to bloom but is very long-lived; some specimens in the UK are now 140 years old, dating from Hooker's introductions from Sikkim in 1849. Also found in East Nepal and Bhutan. Grown from wild or hand-pollinated seed or grafted. Fairly readily obtainable but only suitable for the more favoured sheltered woodland gardens where it should be given plenty of room to develop.

Ssp. *eximium* is very closely related but usually of slightly smaller stature with a more flat-topped habit. The superb leaves, with rusty indumentum on both the upper and lower surface, are especially attractive as they unfurl. The flowers are usually pink fading to cream.

FASTIGIATUM (Lapponica SS)

H5 dwarf April–May 5/6a

This dwarf blue species is one of the easiest of all species to grow, and is deservedly very popular, as are its numerous hybrids such as 'INTRIFAST' and 'RAMAPO'. It covers itself with flowers of light-to-deep blue-purple, on a very neat compact bush, usually with attractive tiny glaucous leaves. Easy to root, readily available, extremely free-flowering, and hardy enough for any British garden, preferring a site in full sun. Found in south-west China. The name meaning 'erect' is not satisfactory for such a compact plant.

falconeri ssp. *eximium* C&H 427

IMPEDITUM is virtually identical to the above, apart from certain near-microscopic botanical features; many plants commercially available as *impeditum* are in fact *fastigiatum*. The main discernible difference is that most forms of *impeditum* have greenish rather than bluish leaves.

ORTHOCLADUM VAR. MICROLEUCUM is a very hardy, dense, dwarf species with tiny leaves and masses of frost-hardy, small, pure-white flowers. A good contrast to the blue-purple of the above. April–May. A.M. 1939.

FERRUGINEUM (Rhododendron SS)

H5 dwarf-semi dwarf June–July 5/6a

The well-known Alpenrose from the Alps and Pyrenees. Being native to Europe, it is not surprising that it has been in cultivation in Britain since 1740. R. *ferrugineum* is especially useful as one of the latest to flower of all dwarfs, producing its clusters of small rosy-crimson to pink flowers as late as July in some forms. Not as spectacular as many of the early-flowering dwarfs, but a good form can put on an impressive show. A neat dense compact plant in full sun, with healthy deep-green leaves which in some forms have wavy edges. Very hardy, and being late in flower its flowers are not vulnerable to late spring frosts, so it can be recommended for any British garden. White forms also exist, which in our experience are harder to grow than the pink forms, but are worth trying for variation.

HIRSUTUM is closely related to the above, and found wild above limestone. It differs from *ferrugineum* in its paler flowers and its hairy foliage, reflected in its name. Useful for having a degree of lime-tolerance, it is worth trying in soils thought unsuitable for rhododendrons. We also grow a double flowered form 'Flore Pleno' which is attractive in flower, but needs extra care in its cultivation, as does the occasionally seen white form.

FORMOSUM (Maddenia SS)

H2/3 medium April–June 7b/8a–7a

One of the hardier members of the tender Maddenia subsection; we risk growing this outside on a wall, but keep other plants inside in case of hard winters. Scented flowers are white, sometimes pink- or yellow-tinged or striped red outside, in trusses of 2–3, on an upright sometimes straggly bush with small hairy leaves. An excellent plant outdoors in southern and western gardens. It also makes a fine pot-plant for a conservatory.

FORMOSUM var. INAEQUALE H1/2 (8b–7b/8a). Similar to the above, but with larger leaves and flowers and a much stronger scent. Unfortunately it is not as hardy as *formosum* and is only growable outdoors in the most favourable Cornish and western Scottish gardens. Worth growing as a greenhouse plant if you have room, for its superb scent and fine flowers. Not widely available.

JOHNSTONEANUM H2–3 (7b/8a–7a). Another of the hardier Maddenia species, worth growing outside in moderately cold gardens. In a sheltered site at Glendoick, only severest winters damage the hardier forms. Slightly fragrant flowers are usually creamy-yellow, sometimes flushed pink. Some forms are double or semi-double. A rather rangy bush which benefits from pruning. Quite widely available.

forrestii Repens R. 59174

FORRESTII (Neriiflora SS)

H4 dwarf-semi dwarf March–May 6b

The parent of some of the most popular hybrids ever raised, including 'ELIZABETH' and 'SCARLET WONDER', unfortunately the species itself in its various forms is hard to grow well, and needs extra care. Named after the famous plant collector George Forrest who discovered and introduced many of our best Rhododendron species. Several different subgroups exist, but all have fleshy scarlet to crimson flowers and deep-green rounded leaves, on compact dense spreading plants. To grow at its best, it should be in the open but in a moist, cool, well-drained site, a north-facing bank being ideal. Kept free of weeds, and planted in groups which will join up and carpet the ground, the effect is very fine. Flowers and growth often rather early so worth protecting with a cloche in late April and early May if frost is forecast. Some forms are decidedly shy-flowering, and it is worth seeking out the best clones. Undoubtedly most successful in cooler northern gardens, where there is less chance of burning or drying out in the sun. ***R. forrestii*** **Repens** is the most popular group, with a low creeping habit. The best form we have seen is a clone of **Rock 59174**, which has large bright-scarlet flowers and is relatively free-flowering for this species. ***R. forrestii*** **Tumescens** is a mounding plant which grows taller than Repens.

CHAMAE-THOMSONII is a larger-growing version of *forrestii*, up to 3 ft (1 m) in some forms, with similar red flowers to the above. **Var. *chamaethauma*** has pink flowers. Generally freer-flowering than *forrestii* with more flowers to the truss but overall a coarser plant.

FORTUNEI (Fortunea SS)

H5 medium-tall May–June 5

Named after Robert Fortune, who collected some of the most important Rhododendron species in China during the 19th century, this is a fine scented species which has been much used in hybridizing to produce 'LODERI', 'SCINTILLATION' and many others. Open-topped trusses of fragrant white or lilac-white flowers, often tinged pink, up to 3in (7.6 cm) across. Large smooth pale-green leaves with a purple leaf stalk on an upright, tough, vigorous plant which will grow very large under good conditions. This is the hardiest scented species, and is suitable for any British garden though the leaf size and somewhat early growth require shelter. 'Mrs Butler' is a well-known pink clone. **Ssp. *discolor*** is a June–July flowering form of the species with longer, narrower leaves, also much used in hybridizing. It is hard to find good forms of ssp. *discolor* in the UK.

FULGENS (Fulgenia SS)

H3–4 medium-tall February–April 7a–6b

A fine early-flowering species from the Himalayas, with blood-red to bright-scarlet flowers in neat, rounded trusses. A compact grower, with rounded leaves, indumented below, with the additional attraction of smooth peeling pinkish-red bark, and crimson leaf bracts on the young growth. Although hardy enough for sheltered gardens in most of Britain, its early flowering demands a favourable site to avoid regular frost damage. Widely available.

SUCCOTHII is a closely related species, which has no indumentum on the leaf underside. Shorter leaf-stalks, and the leaves are often upward pointing. Flowers similar to those of *fulgens*. Rather susceptible to powdery mildew.

FULVUM (Fulva SS)

H3–4 medium-tall March–April 7a–6b

This is a fine, large species suitable for woodland gardens in all but the harshest of British climates. Although young plants are prone to damage from spring frosts, we find this a reliable long-lived plant at Glendoick. Compact trusses of white to rose flowers, usually blotched crimson. Dark-green leaves, up to 10in (25cm) long, with fine tawny to reddish indumentum below, on an upright bush which will form a small tree. Collected by Forrest, Ludlow and Sherriff, and others from Yunnan, Burma, Tibet and Northern India. Freer-flowering from a younger age than most of the large growing indumented species, this is a good choice for starting a collection of more unusual larger growers. Quite widely available.

UVARIFOLIUM is a related species with a paler thinner indumentum, usually white to fawn. This is a variable species, some forms having rather poor flowers, but two fine clones are quite widely available in the UK, which we would recommend. **'Yangtze Bend'** A.M. has pink flowers, while **'Reginald Childs'** A.M. has white flowers, suffused rose and blotched deeper, with particularly fine foliage.

GLAUCOPHYLLUM (Glauca SS)

H3–4 low late April–May 7a–6b

A low-growing species, ideal for the back of a border of dwarf rhododendrons or the edge of a woodland garden, forming a bush usually wider than high, up to 4 by 6ft (1.2 by 2cm) in a favourable site. Pinkish-purple to pink or white flowers in clusters of 4–10. Loose to compact to habit with very aromatic leaves, white underneath, and attractive peeling bark. The pink and purple forms are hardy enough for most areas of Britain, although somewhat vulnerable to spring frosts, but we find the white forms more tender and harder to

fulvum

uvarifolium 'Yangtze Bend' A.M.

griersonianum

please. Moderately easy to root and usually available. **Var. *tubiforme*** has more tubular flowers, and is generally more bud tender. Several related species can also be recommended:

CHARITOPES has very attractive clear apple-blossom-pink flowers. Not as hardy as *glaucophyllum* and rather bud tender.

LUTEIFLORUM although rather bud and plant tender, has lovely lemon-yellow flowers. Our own hybrid 'TEAL' is an easier grown alternative.

GRIERSONIANUM (Griersoniana SS)

H(2)/3 low-medium June–July (7b/8a)–7a

Discovered by George Forrest in 1917 in Yunnan, China, this species has proven to be one of the most useful parents in hybridizing, producing 'ELIZABETH', 'VANESSA PASTEL', 'VULCAN', 'FABIA' and many others. It imparts to its offspring extreme freedom of flowering from a young age and pure colours without a bluish cast. Its one drawback is its tendency to grow very late in the season, often into September and October, resulting in damage from the first frosts in many areas, and unfortunately this problem is passed on to many of its offspring which habitually produce late second growth. Loose trusses of bright geranium-scarlet flowers on a rangy, straggly bush with long thin leaves with a pale indumentum below. Although rather tender, it seems to recover well from frost damage, and tolerates shadier, drier conditions than most species, so is worth trying in borderline districts in a favourable site. We only lost it in our severest winters of 1981/1982. Very successful in southern and western coastal gardens, where it can be pruned hard into a compact shape. Easy to root, and quite widely available.

GRIFFITHIANUM (Fortunea SS)

H2/(3) tall May 7b/8a(–7a)

The background parent to many of the most popular large-flowered Dutch, English, and American hybrids which are everyone's idea of the typical rhododendron. 'PINK PEARL', 'JEAN MARIE DE MONTAGUE', 'LODERI' and many others owe their large flowers to *griffithianum*. Unfortunately the species itself is very tender and is only really successful in favourable western and south-coast gardens, although it may be kept alive elsewhere in a very favourable site. It has almost the largest flowers of any species, up to 3in by 6in (7.6cm–15cm) in size, white or white tinged pink or yellowish, with green spots on base, in trusses of 3–6, and with the bonus of scent in most forms. In a sheltered favourable site, it will form a tree over 20ft (6m) high with long smooth leaves and an attractive peeling bark. Found wild in Himalayan forests, and named after D. Griffith who first found it.

HAEMATODES (Neriiflora SS)

H4 semi-dwarf-low May–June 6b

One of the finest smaller red-flowered species for flower and foliage. Fleshy, scarlet-to-crimson (the name means 'blood-like'), tubular flowers on a compact bush with dark leathery leaves, covered below with a thick woolly rufous indumentum. Wild in western Yunnan where we saw it as an under-shrub, creeping about below larger rhododendrons. In cultivation, it is best grown on a fairly open site to maintain its compact habit and it hates soggy soil which can cause it to collapse and die. Quite readily obtainable and fairly easy to root. Takes about 7–10 years to bloom from seed. Quite variable as to leaf size, colour of indumentum and to colour of calyx which can be red or green. The parent of many hybrids such as 'HUMMINGBIRD' and 'MAY DAY'.

haematodes

insigne

HIPPOPHAEOIDES (Lapponica SS)

H5 semi dwarf-low April–May 5/6a

This is one of the hardiest and easiest grown dwarfs, with relatively frost-resistant flowers, and is suitable for any UK garden. Lavender-blue flowers from a young age on a generally upright bush with greyish-green foliage. Found on the moorlands of western China where it has been found growing in very boggy ground or even in water. Not always easy to root but easily layered. Readily available commercially in several forms, two of the best being **Bei-ma-shan**, rather tall with the best lavender-blue flowers, and **Yu 13845**, lower, with neater habit and paler flowers.

LAPPONICUM Parvifolium is the Siberian or Japanese form of this normally Arctic species. The earliest to flower of the Lapponicums, from January to March, with magenta-rose to purple flowers which are remarkably frost-hardy, making *lapponicum* a very useful small, winter-flowering shrub. Hard to root and best layered.

INSIGNE (Argyrophylla SS)

H5 low-medium May–June 6a

An excellent hardy species with loose-to-rounded trusses of 8–16 flowers, pinkish white to deep pink, with crimson spotting and rose-coloured lines. While the flowers are attractive, this species is most outstanding for its foliage. It has thick, grooved, rigid-pointed leaves with an indumentum below which has an unusual metallic sheen, sometimes described as like 'burnished copper'. If grown in plenty of light, it will form a well-shaped dense bush which looks good all the year round, and which is free-flowering once established. Its merits have attracted this species to German hybridizers, and in the next few years some of their results will become available in Britain. The name means 'remarkable' and it was introduced from west Sichuan, China by E. H. Wilson in 1908. A good plant for all UK gardens, and one of the finest foliage species suitable for severest areas.

ARGYROPHYLLUM, in its various forms, is closely related. White to deep rose-pink flowers on a taller bush than *insigne*. The indumentum is usually a striking silvery to white colour. Not as hardy, and earlier-flowering than *insigne*. The most popular clone in the UK is **ssp. *nankingense* 'Chinese Silver'** A. M. Pink flowers and fine white indumentum.

argyrophyllum

IRRORATUM (Irrorata SS)

H3–4 low-medium early
March–May 7a–6b

A very variable species from Yunnan, China, which is very fine in its best forms and decidedly average in its poorer ones. Freely produced flowers in loose trusses, white, yellowish to various shades of pink, sometimes unspotted and sometimes spotted very heavily. The foliage is usually not particulary striking. Not suitable for colder gardens and needs shelter. **'Polka Dot'** A.M. is probably the most popular clone, with light-pink flowers, very heavily spotted purple. This may in fact be a hybrid, and some people find it rather gaudy. We also recommend the better pure white forms, of which there are several. The pinker forms are better chosen in flower, as some are rather muddy, but good ones exist.

irroratum 'Polka Dot' A.M.

morii RV. 71001

MORII (Maculifera SS) is similar in appearance to the above, and is one of the most free-flowering of all species. Generally hardier than *irroratum* although some forms come into growth early, so are frost-vulnerable. Flowering in April–May, its loose trusses range from pink to white, with a range of markings and spotting. Very successful in a sheltered site, and worthy of more widespread cultivation. Named after U. Mori who first collected it in its native Taiwan.

KEISKEI (Triflora SS)

H5 dwarf April–May 5/6a

The hardiest and most dwarf member of the Triflora subsection, it is named after Keisuke Ito who discovered it in Japan. Pale-to-lemon-yellow flowers freely produced. Although it exists in many different forms, there are only two worth general cultivation outside specialist collections. The semi-dwarf forms, the best of which is '**Ebino**', have reddish bronzy winter colour and young growth, on compact plants growing no more than 12in (30.5cm) high at Glendoick. The other type is **var. *cordifolia*** the best of which is '**Yaku Fairy**' A.M. 1970. This is one of the lowest-growing and most compact of all dwarfs, forming an impenetrable mat a few inches high. It covers itself with relatively large pale lemon-yellow flowers, completely hiding the foliage. Its later flowering makes it more useful for colder districts than the taller forms. 'Yaku Fairy' is proving to be one of the best of all parents for dwarf hybrids, producing 'GINNY GEE', 'PATTY BEE' and 'TOO BEE', and many more offspring are in the pipeline. 'Yaku Fairy' is

keiskei 'Yaku Fairy' A.M.

very hardy and will grow well in full exposure in even the coldest UK gardens.

HANCEANUM is a similar species. The A.M. form has creamy flowers on a low-growing bush with striking bronzy new growth. **'Nanum'** is a very dwarf form with deep-yellow flowers which is very slow-growing, and really a collector's plant.

KELETICUM (Saluenensia SS)

H4–5 dwarf May–June 6b–5/6a

One of the latest-flowering dwarf species, and so a very useful addition to a collection. Pale to deep crimson-purple flowers, usually flat-faced and held above the foliage. Easy to grow, free-flowering and vigorous, with a creeping or mounding habit, and good for ground cover. Hardy anywhere in the UK, and should be planted in full sun. Plants from **Rock 58** have particularly fine flowers. Easy to root and widely available.

RADICANS GROUP has deep-green, shiny leaves, the smallest of any rhododendron, about a quarter-inch (0.5cm) in length. A favourite for rock-garden enthusiasts, forming a dense pin-cushion or creeping bush which roots to the ground, growing only a few inches high. Relatively large flat-faced purple flowers on long stalks in late May and June. Hardy in the whole of the UK but not always happy; does best planted in a little shade in a sloping peat bed. The most dwarf forms should be sought out, as it merges with typical *keleticum* and taller intermediate forms are not so striking. Easy to root and readily available.

LACTEUM (Taliensia SS)

H4 low-medium April–May 6b

This species presents a real challenge for the enthusiast; it has some of the finest yellow flowers of any species, but making it happy is no easy task. Large trusses of 15–30 flowers of pale-to-clear canary yellow, sometimes blotched crimson. A rather slow-growing bush, leaves rounded at the ends, with a thin brown indumentum below. Very fastidious as to conditions, it seems to like some shade, very good drainage, and very acid soil, and does best in drier, cooler gardens on the eastern side of the UK. Grafted plants may be easier to please, but do not accept them if PONTICUM has been used as an understock. It is very variable in flower, and good forms should be sought out, as many seedlings from cultivated plants turn out to be rather pinkish and muddy. There are many excellent clones, alas very hard to obtain commercially. The best of all is probably **'Blackhills'** F.C.C. 1965 which is virtually unobtainable. There are also new introductions from China which so far look healthier than normal. At the time of writing these are too young to flower. The name means 'milky' but the most desirable forms are of a more yellow shade than the name suggests. Hardy in almost any garden, a first class plant if you can grow it, and much used as a parent, unfortunately passing on its miffyness to its offspring. The best-known is probably 'LIONEL'S TRIUMPH'.

LEPIDOSTYLUM (Trichoclada SS)

H4–5 dwarf-semi dwarf June 6b–6a

This dwarf species, from Yunnan and Burma, is grown mainly for its striking bristly blue-green leaves, especially attractive in the early summer, for which it received an A.M. The yellow flowers are rather small and insignificant, and do not seem to blend with the foliage. Normally hardy in any UK garden but damaged in some places in the 1981/82 winters. Low-growing, dense and compact, best grown in full sun, in clumps of several plants if you have room.

MEKONGENSE VIRIDESCENS is a closely related species, taller than the above (up to 4 ft [1.2m]) but with similar glaucous foliage. The late yellow flowers are more striking than those of *lepidostylum*. **'Doshong La'** A.M. is a good clone, selected by ourselves, and named after the mountain pass where it was collected by F. Kingdon Ward. Easy to please, and useful for its June–July flowering, it should be hardy enough for any UK garden. **'Rubroluteum'** is a variation of the above with reddish tinges to the flowers.

◄ *lacteum*

lindleyi

LINDLEYI (Maddenia SS)

H2–3 low-medium late
April–May 7b/8a–7a

From the eastern Himalayas, this is one of the very best of the scented Maddenii species, and in its hardiest forms it is worth trying outdoors even in gardens as cold as Glendoick. Elsewhere it will make a fine cool-greenhouse or conservatory shrub. Here it flowers outside on a wall or in a protected woodland and is only killed in our severest winters. The hardier forms are very successful outside in western Scotland and south-west England. Usually 3–7 flower trusses, white, with a yellow base, often tinged pink, resembling a trumpet lily, strongly scented; 'nutmeg and lemon' is how T. Moore describes it. A rangy, straggly grower which is best in a clump, allowing the shoots to form a tangled thicket, or on a stump, wall, or mossy tree. Very free-flowering from a young age, and often a show-winner in its best forms. Plants from **L&S 6562** are hardier than most other introductions, and these should be sought for colder gardens.

DALHOUSIAE is a related species with large showy flowers, opening greenish-yellow and fading to cream. Only for greenhouses or milder districts, and also rather straggly. **Var. *rhabdotum*** has bold red stripes down each flower, and looks quite unlike any other rhododendron.

NUTTALLII is the giant of the Maddenia species in size of plant, foliage and flower. Huge heavily textured white to creamy-yellow flowers, often tinged pink, yellow or orange. Alas, not really hardy enough for anywhere in the UK out of doors, so a greenhouse or conservatory plant.

lutescens 'Bagshot Sands' A.M.

LUTESCENS (Triflora SS)

H3–4 medium March 7a–6b

The Triflorums are a group of mainly tall-growing, small-leaved species with flowers of many different colours and *lutescens* is the most spectacular yellow-flowered member of the subsection. Three-flower trusses of flat-faced pale-to-deeper-primrose yellow flowers, spotted green. A tall straggly grower which benefits from pruning, especially in shade. The best forms of the species have very striking bronzy-red young growth which sometimes persists all summer. Unfortunately most of the hardiest forms have small flowers, and the best of the named clones are rather tender. The F.C.C. clone has large flowers and excellent red growth but we find it particularly vulnerable to spring frosts, and we would recommend it only for western and southern gardens. We find **'Bagshot Sands'** A.M. to be somewhat hardier, and more suitable for colder gardens. These clones are probably not worth attempting in gardens much colder than Glendoick. Free-flowering, easy to root and readily available.

MACABEANUM (Grandia SS)

H3–4 tall March–May 7a–6b

Native to north-east India, this is one of the finest large-leaved species of all. Hardier than most of its relations, it can be grown in a favourable woodland site in most lowland British gardens. Yellow to yellowish-white flowers, blotched purple, in a large stacked truss of up to 30. Leaves up to 12in (30cm) long are shiny above and have a white or fawn, compacted, woolly indumentum below. The large red growth buds open out like candles to silvery upwards-pointing

maddenii

shoots, with red bud scales, and this is a show in itself. A giant grower, especially in western gardens, it has attained 30ft (9m) in some places. Much slower-growing where there is less rainfall. It takes some years to flower, but on the whole will start blooming younger than its relatives, and is more tolerant of less-than-ideal conditions. Some forms are poor with floppy trusses and pale flowers, but many superb ones exist and it is worth seeking them out.

PRAESTANS H4 (6b) is one of the hardiest large-leaved species, and with wind shelter, it can do well in quite severe climates. It has interesting dark leaves, shiny below, with a wide, flattened leaf-stalk. Flowers white to magenta-rose, usually early.

MADDENII (Maddenia SS)

H2–3 medium-tall May–July 7b/8a–7a

A very variable species, formerly grown under various names such as *polyandrum*, *brachysiphon*, *manipurense* etc. White through cream to pink or even light-purple flowers, sometimes with darker lines or base, waxy and sweetly scented. Tough, leathery dark-green leaves, small to large, on an erect-to-sprawling plant of varying heigl and vigour. The type plant from the Himalayas is generally too tender for all but the mildest British gardens and the stronger-growing forms are too large for pot culture.

Ssp. *crassum* from China is often a little hardier and is worth attempting in favourable sheltered southern and eastern gardens in addition to those on the west coast where this is very successful. Also variable in foliage, habit and flower. Useful for its late, scented flowers but these are easily damaged by hot or wet weather. Cuttings root fairly easily. Not often available.

MALLOTUM (Neriiflora SS)

H3–4 low February–April 7a–6b

Discovered by F. Kingdon Ward on the Burma-Yunnan frontier in 1914, this is a superb medium-sized species at its best, but unfortunately its early flowers are often frosted. Probably not suitable for gardens colder than Glendoick as we nearly lost it in the 1981/82 winter. Waxy crimson to scarlet or rosy-scarlet flowers in a compact rounded truss. Excellent foliage; the leaves, up to 7in (18cm) long, rounded at the ends, are deep green, and have thick, woolly, cinnamon-brown indumentum below. An upright but fairly compact grower, which makes a fine specimen if not in too much shade. Needs a sheltered, frost-drained site to do well, and worth a prime position, as it is such a fine foliage plant. Leaves suffer insect damage in some gardens. Quite a uniform species, most forms are good, successful grafted or raised from hand-pollinated seed. Fairly widely available.

MOUPINENSE (Moupinensia SS)

H3–4 low January–March 7a–6b

One of the earliest species to flower, sometimes opening in January at Glendoick, and the flowers can withstand a few degrees of frost, producing a show in most years. The beautiful, freely produced flowers range from white to pale and deep pink, with or without spots, in trusses of 1–3. The colour intensity is affected by the weather, being deeper after a cold spell. Small stiff deep-green leaves on an upright but normally fairly compact bush that often needs support from a wall or stakes to avoid it flopping over. It is a very brittle plant, prone to breaking off at the rootball, especially when young, and is prone to bark split from spring frosts. We find our white form more tender than the pink. R. *moupinense* needs perfect drainage, and is tolerant of dry sites, so can be planted nearer to greedy trees, but not in too much shade. Found in Sichuan, China, often as an epiphyte (growing on a tree), and it was introduced by E. Wilson in 1909. It has been used as a parent of early-flowering hybrids such as 'BO PEEP', 'SETA' and 'TESSA'.

moupinense

NERIIFLORUM (Neriiflora SS)

H3–4 low-medium April–May 7a–6b

This is a very variable species found wild across a large area of south-west China and Upper Burma. Freely produced bright scarlet to crimson flowers, 5–12 per usually loose truss. The smooth leaves, usually glaucous below, on a bush normally fairly compact in sun, but which can get very straggly in shade. It is hard to find the best hardy forms of this species, but new forms have been introduced from the wild recently that may prove to be good. Not very hardy with us, and does best further south and west, but worth a try in colder gardens as it is a showy plant at its best. Plants sold as 'Euchaites' are often taller-growing than the type. Reasonable availability.

NIVEUM (Arborea SS)

H3–4 medium April–May 7a–6b

Not everyone's favourite colour, but a very fine species in its best forms, contrasting well with yellows but not so well with reds. Around 20-flower, rounded trusses of smokey blue/purple to lavender and mauve. The colour in the best forms of this species is unique amongst rhododendrons, but some of the magenta forms are not attractive. Deeply grooved thick leaves have a near white indumentum below, and this is especially attractive as a downy covering as the new leaves unfurl (hence the name which means 'snow-like'). Rarely damaged at Glendoick. Native to Bhutan and Sikkim, and said to be rare in the wild, although new forms have been recently introduced. Quite readily available commercially.

◄ *niveum*

LANIGERUM Closely related but with pink to scarlet-crimson flowers. The very large rounded flower buds open early and are easily damaged. Fine foliage is very similar to that of *niveum*. Well worth growing in favoured gardens. There are several good award forms, the most commonly available being **'Chapel Wood'** F.C.C.

ORBICULARE (Fortunea SS)

H4 low-medium April–May 6b

A distinctive species from Sichuan province, China, very easily recognized by its more or less round (orbicular) bright-green leaves with clefts at the base. Bell-shaped flowers in a loose truss of 7–10 are rose-deep pink through purplish pink. Some forms have very poor pendulous and/or bluish-pink flowers, and these should be avoided in favour of the best pink forms. Hardy in most of the UK and needs plenty of light and space to avoid a tendency to straggliness. A very worthwhile foliage plant when grown as a dense bush, and much larger in all parts than the rather similar dwarf species WILLIAMSIANUM. These two species have been crossed to produce the hybrid 'TEMPLE BELLE'.

orbiculare

oreodoxa var. *fargesii*

OREODOXA (Fortunea SS)

H4–5 medium March–April 6b–6a

One of the most free-flowering, versatile and reliable of the early-flowering species; its remarkably frost-resistant buds enable it to put on some sort of show virtually every year. Flowers range from white to shades of pink and pale lilac, sometimes spotted, in loose trusses of 6–12. Smooth oval leaves on a vigorous bush which forms a small tree. This will survive with less shelter than most of the early-flowering species, so is useful for exposed gardens. The leaves are very sensitive to cold and heat, curling up quicker than any other species but not harming them in any way. The name means 'glory of the mountains' and the species is found over a very large area of north-west China. The closely related **var. *fargesii*** is particularly useful as it can tolerate poor clay soils. Widely available in both forms.

VERNICOSUM is a similar species with fine flowers of pale pink, rose-lavender to bright rose in a fuller truss. Usually later-flowering and not quite as tough as *oreodoxa*, benefitting from more shelter. Easy, free-flowering and usually available.

PACHYSANTHUM (Maculifera SS)

H4 low-medium April 6b

This is one of the most important post-war new species introductions. It was first introduced from Taiwan in 1972, and first flowered in cultivation at Glendoick in 1979. It is one of the finest foliage-plants in the genus—its pointed leaves have a thick buff-to-brown indumentum below with a striking silvery-to-brown tomentum above which persists through the summer. A fairly compact grower, our largest plants are now about 5ft by 5ft (1.5m by 1.5m) in 15 years. The flowers are in quite well-filled trusses, white to pink, spotted or blotched green or red. Seems to be perfectly hardy here so far, maybe deserving an H5 (5/6a) rating, and should be hardy almost anywhere in Britain, although its rather early flowers are vulnerable in colder gardens. One of our favourite species, and well worth a place in any collection. Becoming more readily available.

PEMAKOENSE (Uniflora SS)

H4 dwarf March–April 6b

This is one of the most free-flowering of all dwarfs, but unfortunately the swelling buds are very frost-tender, often preventing its spectacular display. A very dwarf spreading grower which forms a dense mat with a suckering habit. Small shiny leaves are hidden by the pinkish-purple to near-pink, relatively large flowers. Apart from its frost-tender flowers, this is an easy plant to please, best in an open position and suitable for anywhere comparable or less severe than Glendoick. Named after the province of Pemako in Tibet where it was first collected by F. Kingdon Ward. A parent of the hybrids 'SNIPE', 'PHALAROPE', 'ROSE ELF' which are not quite so bud-tender.

PONTICUM (Pontica SS)

H4 medium May–June 6b

The infamous 'wild' species is so well known it hardly needs describing. A vigorous, invasive shrub with shiny leaves, which opens its lilac/purplish-pink, often spotted flowers, in late May and June. This is now a serious environmental pest in west-coast and southern parts of the UK, where the rainfall is higher than average. It spreads by layers and seed, and we would not recommend planting it in such areas. On the east side of the UK, it is a very useful windbreak, hedge and general background plant, and is much used as cover for shooting. It is growable in drier, shadier and damper conditions than most other species, and so can be planted in the least favourable sites, though it can suffer frost damage in colder areas. Not a British native, although it may have been before the last Ice Age, it has a scattered distribution around the southern parts of the Black Sea, Lebanon and the southern Iberian Peninsula and was introduced to Britain in the 1770s. A form of the Turkish *ponticum*, rare in the UK, was collected in 1962 under AC&H 205. This has produced far more handsome plants than the typical form, with deep-green foliage and deep-purple flowers. Several garden forms of *ponticum* also exist with odd foliage variations. The best known, sometimes known as 'Silver Edge', is **'Ponticum Variegatum'** a less vigorous compact upright grower with narrow leaves, edged creamy white. Flowers purple.

CATAWBIENSE H5 (5) is a related species from north America. Hardier and far less invasive than *ponticum*. It and some of its hybrids make better background plants than *ponticum* where the latter is too vigorous or too tender. One of the hardiest of all species and part of the parentage of most of the toughest hardy hybrids. Flowers light to dark purplish pink, occasionally white. June. Readily available.

MACROPHYLLUM is a species from west of the Rockies, USA; it is a rather straggly, usually upright grower, with average foliage and bright pink to purple or rarely white flowers. May–June. Has the advantage of being very drought-resistant, and can be planted on steep banks and other sites too dry for other rhododendrons. Not good in dense shade, as it becomes very leggy and shy-flowering. Sometimes available.

pseudochrysanthum

PSEUDOCHRYSANTHUM (Maculifera SS)

H4–5 dwarf-medium April–May 6b–6a

An excellent Taiwanese species with very distinctive foliage; leaves on very short stalks are thick, rigid and pointed, often covered in a thin white indumentum on the young growth. Loose trusses of 5–10 white to pale-pink flowers, spotted within, opening from pink buds. Very variable in size, ranging from 10ft (3m) to very dwarf. The latter, from RV 72003, are only a few inches high at Glendoick, and are marvellous foliage plants, although the smallest still have not flowered after 16 years. The species is rather prone to leaf-tip burning, and this seems to be best avoided by light shade and by cutting back on fertilizer. Hardy and suitable for all but the very severest gardens. An excellent, thoroughly recommended species. Many good forms are in the trade. The A.M. clone is a larger growing one with white flowers, flushed pink and spotted crimson.

MACULIFERUM ssp. ANHWEIENSE is a very hardy species from the eastern Chinese province of Anhui. Makes a compact, rounded shrub of low to medium stature with rather pale-green foliage. The freely produced pale-pink-spotted flowers in a fairly loose truss are particularly frost resistant. Usually available.

maculiferum ssp. *anhweiense* ➤

racemosum 'Rock Rose' A.M.

RACEMOSUM (Scabrifolia SS)

H3–4(5) semi dwarf-medium
March–May 7a–6b(5/6a)

The flowers of this species are produced in racemes (hence the name), meaning that unlike most species it flowers along the stems as well as at the terminals or ends of the shoots. Deep-rose to pink and sometimes white flowers, in multiple clusters up the stems, produce a spectacular show in the best forms. Small leaves, often reddish when young, on reddish stems, on an upright plant. In habit, it is very variable, ranging from compact, to tall, rangy and straggly, the latter benefitting from pruning of the long shoots after they have finished flowering. The hardiest forms should be suitable for all but the severest UK gardens, but these are not always commercially available in the UK. Many poor forms abort many of their flower buds and these should be avoided. Some good forms include: **'Glendoick'**—raised here, a tall grower with particularly deep-coloured flowers; **'Rock Rose'** A.M.—bright-pink flowers, also tall; the most widely available clone in the UK; **'Whitelace'** A.M.—very straggly but with fine white flowers; **Forrest 19404** is a dwarf pink. R. *racemosum* is quite tolerant of dry conditions and has relatively frost-resistant flowers. Fairly easy to root, very free-flowering and widely available. The parent of many hybrids, including 'ANNA BALDSIEFEN', 'EGRET', 'GINNY GEE', 'ROSE ELF', and many others.

rex ssp. *fictolacteum*

REX (Falconera SS)

H4 tall April–May 6b

This is the hardiest and easiest to grow of the large-leaved species with indumentum, though it does require wind shelter. It certainly lives up to its name meaning 'The King'. Hardy in all but the coldest UK gardens. The 20–30 flower trusses range from white to pink and mauve-pink, usually with crimson spotting or blotching. Deep-green leaves, up to 18in (46cm) long, have a heavy buff-coloured indumentum below. An extremely fine foliage plant which needs plenty of room.

Ssp. *fictolacteum* is closely related but generally slightly smaller in all parts. The indumentum is usually darker than the above, rust-brown or even chocolate-coloured. The flowers are more variable in colour with more spotting or blotching. Although both these take several years to bloom, they are so impressive out of flower that the flowers are an added bonus. We would recommend these as the first large-leaved species to try; they are deservedly popular and widely available. Many good forms exist, which are occasionally available as grafted specimens. There are fine seedlings from new introductions from Yunnan, and it is also successful from hand-pollinated seed provided the best forms are used in the pollinating.

hodgsonii

HODGSONII, a Himalayan species, is almost as hardy as the above. The impressive foliage has a rather metallic look above when young and the coloured peeling bark is very handsome. The flower colour varies from pink to deep magenta when first open, fading out to near cream. There have been many new introductions recently from Nepal and Bhutan. Commonly available.

KESANGIAE is a newly described species from Bhutan now becoming available. Large handsome leaves and rounded buds, in contrast to the pointed buds of *hodgsonii*. Rough bark. The fine trusses are deep rose to pale pink. It is likely to prove almost as hardy as *hodgsonii* and, like R. *rex*, will need shelter.

roxieanum Oreonastes

ROXIEANUM OREONASTES Group (Taliensia SS)

H5 semi dwarf-low April–May 6a

The Oreonastes forms of *roxieanum* are some of the most attractive and unusual of all dwarf species for foliage. Long thin dark-green leaves, indumented below, radiate from the dense to upright-growing bush giving an effect like the quills of a porcupine. The striking flowers take several years to appear; full rounded trusses of white, sometimes flushed rose, with crimson spots. Perfectly hardy throughout the UK, and although it grows most compactly in full sun, we find that it is freer-flowering with a little shade and shelter. Very hard to root, so must be grafted or raised from hand-pollinated seed: the latter method we find very effective, as long as the best forms of the species are used. Quite widely available and recommended.

PROTEOIDES is a connoisseurs' plant, related to the above, and another member of the Taliensia subsection, so beloved by rhodoholics. It is mainly grown for its tiny neat foliage and woolly indumentum on a very dwarf, compact, slow-growing bush. Hard to root, rarely flowers and rare, so demand always exceeds supply. See ADENOGYNUM for other related species.

RECURVOIDES *Glischra* SS is a similar species with small flat trusses of pink and white flowers. Mainly grown for its outstanding foliage and habit. Bristly, long deep-green leaves, with a tawny/cinnamon to greenish indumentum below, on a very compact plant of 2–4ft (0.6–1.2m). Hardy but rather early into growth, so avoid a frost pocket.

rubiginosum

RUBIGINOSUM (Heliolepida SS)

H(3)–4 medium-tall March–April (7a)–6b

The most vigorous of all species at Glendoick; we find it ideal as an internal windbreak or very informal hedge. It could be used as a main windbreak in warmer gardens, but it can suffer wind and frost damage in our severe winters. Flowers come in a variety of shades from near-white through lavender/mauve/rose, often with purple, brown, or crimson spots. With this variation, it is worth planting a group or hedge of several forms for the most interesting mass effect. Leaves are scaly, up to about 4in (10cm) long, and the habit is generally upright and willowy. Variable in hardiness, some introductions are tender at Glendoick. R *rubiginosum* now includes what was the species *desquamatum*, although in cultivation, plants sold as *desquamatum* usually have larger, flatter flowers, and are sometimes more compact though generally more tender and earlier into growth. There are many selected clones around, including **'Wakehurst'** A.M. which is probably a hybrid with YUNNANENSE. It is worth checking the hardiness of forms offered if you have a cold garden. Fairly easy to root, free-flowering and easy to grow, even in dry or near-neutral soils. Readily available.

HELIOLEPIS is closely related but is less vigorous and much later flowering in June–August. The foliage is usually amongst the most aromatic of the whole genus but it can be too pungent. The flower-colour range is similar to *rubiginosum*. Limited availability.

RUSSATUM (Lapponica SS)

H4–5 dwarf-low April–May 6b–5/6a

A very variable species grown for its deep indigo-purple flowers, which appear freely in clusters. The rich colours of the best forms are a beautiful contrast with other colours, especially yellow. Paler or reddish forms as usually not worth growing. Not surprisingly, the flowers have attracted hybridizers to use this species, producing among others 'AZURWOLKE', 'PENHEALE BLUE', 'SACKO' and 'SONGBIRD'. Fairly easy to root and free-flowering. It varies from the very compact to the tall and straggly; nurseries offer several well-selected (one hopes) forms. As with most dwarf species, this does best in an open site, in clumps with other dwarfs, forming an undulating display.

POLYCLADUM is a related species with smaller, narrower leaves and pale lavender to rich purple-blue flowers. The F.C.C. and Wisley forms, formally known as *scintillans* ('sparkling'), are the best available, and these have some of the finest flowers, nearest to real blue of all the dwarfs. Tiny leaves on a fairly dense grower; it tends to throw long shoots which benefit from pruning. Hardy throughout the UK, best in full sun, free-flowering and readily available. Recommended.

RUPICOLA var. CHRYSEUM is one of the few yellow-flowered Lapponicums, varying from pale to greenish yellow and makes an excellent contrast to the purple and blue species. Very free-flowering. Not easy to root but can be layered easily. A parent of 'CHIKOR'.

SANGUINEUM (Neriiflora SS)

H4 semi dwarf-low March–May 6b

With a name meaning 'blood-red' it is not surprising that this has fleshy bright-crimson flowers which are in loose trusses of 3–6. A compact bush (can be leggy in shade) with small leaves, indumented below. The flowers, which are often very dark, looking best with the sun

sanguineum var. *haemaleum*

shining through them and may take several years to appear. This species is native to a large area of south-west China and Tibet, where many close relations and subspecies are also found. This and its relations must have excellent drainage, but must not dry out, and they tend to be longer-lived in drier, more eastern gardens. **Var. *DIDYMOIDES*** (*roseotinctum*) is very similar in appearance but with flowers of several colours, usually white or yellow flushed pink or red. **Var. *HAEMALEUM*** has very dark red flowers, nearly black in some forms. **Ssp. *DIDYMUM*** is much later flowering than *sanguineum*, usually June/July, and so useful for extending the season. Very deep-red flowers, sometimes black-red. Unfortunately a very difficult plant to please, often with unstable roots and chlorotic foliage. Perhaps better grafted. Grows best in nearly alkaline soil.

CITRINIFLORUM has a thicker indumentum and yellow or yellow-tinged pink flowers. **Var. *horaeum*** Forrest 21850 has striking orange-shot crimson flowers.

MICROGYNUM has crimson flowers from a relatively early age. Perhaps the easiest to grow.

PARMULATUM has white to pink, usually heavily spotted flowers.

TEMENIUM ssp. *gilvum* 'Cruachan' F.C.C. has yellow flowers.

Most of the above are fairly easy to root, and are quite widely available.

SARGENTIANUM (Pogonanthum Section)

H5 dwarf-semi dwarf April–June 6a

One of the best of the Pogonanthum (Anthopogon) group of species which is characterized by clusters of daphne-like flowers, R. *sargentianum* has cream to pale-yellow flowers in trusses of 5–12, on a very compact bush with small dark-green leaves. A fine very hardy species, good in full sun, it does have a tendency to yellowing of leaves, probably due to over-acidity. Try liming the soil to cure chlorosis. Introduced by E. Wilson from west Sichuan in 1903, and named after C. S. Sargent, a former director of the Arnold Arboretum. Several different forms exist: **'Whitebait'** A.M. has relatively large white flowers; A.M. 1923 is pale-yellow. An American hybrid 'MARICEE' is larger-growing than typical *sargentianum* and is usually easier to grow.

TRICHOSTOMUM Taller-growing and usually less hardy than *sargentianum*, this has similar daphne-like flowers in rounded trusses of white to rose. Some rather indifferent forms exist, with flowers neither pink nor white, and these should be avoided. There are quite a number of named selections, most of which are good. The best known is the rose-flowered **'Collingwood Ingram'** F.C.C.

PRIMULIFLORUM (Cephalanthoides group). **'Doker La'** A.M. is a superb clone with clear pale-pink flowers produced earlier in the season than the similar *trichostomum*.

CEPHALANTHUM has white-to-pink flowers, similar to the above. Crebreflorum Group have pink flowers on a compact bush only 2–3in (5–7.6cm) high. This is a very fine species for the connoisseur, ideal for a peat garden.

All the above are tricky to root, and not too easily grown, so they remain rather scarce in commerce.

sargentianum ►

sinogrande

SINOGRANDE (Grandia SS)

H2–3 tall April–May 7b/8a–7a

One of the giant rhododendron species, well-known for its magnificent elephant's-ear leaves, deep green above with smooth indumentum below, which can be up to 3ft (1m) long. The young growth is usually spectacular, remaining grey and metallic for some time after it unfurls. A very large grower, forming a tree up to 30ft (9m) high and often even more across, but quite slow-growing in areas of low rainfall. Enormous trusses of 20–50 flowers, creamy white to pale yellow, with a crimson blotch. It should be planted in a sheltered woodland site to produce the largest leaves and best growth. Takes many years to flower, and only flowers well every second or third year, but magnificent as a foliage plant, and well worth growing for this alone. At Glendoick, we find it tender as a young plant, but surprisingly hardy as it matures, being killed only by exceptionally cold winters. Probably not worth trying in gardens colder than our own. Recently, new forms have been introduced from Yunnan, China, which may prove hardier than older introductions. Selected clones are occasionally available as grafted plants.

MONTROSEANUM H2–(3) A closely related species (previously called pink *sinogrande* or ***mollyanum***), with leaves up to 18in (45cm) long with whitish indumentum below. The best forms have very fine pink to purplish-pink flowers, blotched crimson. Barely hardy at Glendoick, where it is susceptible to bark-split. One of the best clones is '**Benmore**' F.C.C.—two-toned pink flowers with a small blotch.

SMIRNOWII (Pontica SS)

H5 low-medium May–June 5/6a

A very hardy species which will easily withstand the climate of the coldest UK gardens. The 10–12 flowers form loose but compact trusses of mauve to deep pink, occasionally white. Long convex leaves, indumentum white to pale brown below, with white indumentum on the new growth. Best in full sun, where it forms a dense compact bush. A native of Turkey and south-west USSR, it was first introduced in the late 19th century. Easy, very tough, and one of the best species for cold sites.

smirnowii ➤

souliei deep pink

strigillosum

SOULIEI (Campylocarpa SS)

H4–5 low-medium May 6b–6a

One of our favourite species, it has unusual, open, saucer-shaped flowers, pink; pink flushed rose; or pink opening to white. Rounded leaves, glaucous-blue when young, on a fairly compact bush which can become rather leggy, especially in shade. Free-flowering from about 4 years of age. Very hard to root, and hard to graft; we find it easiest to raise from hand-pollinated seed, and we have introduced pink and white strains. Quite easy to grow at Glendoick, but harder further south and west. It needs very good drainage and is best in a fairly sunny site. Needs some shelter to protect its rather early growth, but seen at its best in colder gardens, and should be hardy enough for almost anywhere in the UK. Named after Père Soulie, a French missionary, who discovered it in Sichuan, China. Closely related to WARDII. Usually available.

STRIGILLOSUM (Maculifera SS)

H3–4 medium February–April 7a–6b

In its best forms this is a fine early-flowering species. Flat-topped trusses of 8–12 deep-red to crimson-scarlet flowers with black-crimson nectar pouches. Easily recognized by the bristles and hairs on its leaf stalks and branches. Convex, drooping leaves are long and thin, usually with indumentum below along the midrib, and it forms a dome-shaped plant if not in too much shade. Early-flowering and often rather early into growth, so not for the coldest gardens or for frost pockets, although it is rarely damaged at Glendoick. The name refers to its bristles, and the species is found in a limited area of Sichuan Province, in China. Quite widely available.

thomsonii

THOMSONII (Thomsonia SS)

H3–4 low-tall March–May 7a–6b

A splendid and deservedly popular species, which is a worthy plant for any collection in all but the very coldest gardens. Deep blood-red to dark wine-red, open-bell-shaped flowers with a red to pale-green calyx, in a loose truss of 6–12. Thick rounded leaves up to 3in (7.6cm) long are often a striking glaucous blue when young. Forms an upright tree in most forms, showing off its usually fine peeling but smooth bark. Variable in flower and foliage. Not very easy to root so it is usually grown from seed, although selected forms are sometimes available. It is found in the Himalayas, and several new collections have been made in recent years. Takes some years to flower, but once established, it is free-flowering and reliable, but it does benefit from thorough dead-heading as it will often produce masses of seed. A popular parent and although few of its offspring have proven to be commercial hybrids, many such as '**Shilsoni**' and 'CORNISH CROSS' are often seen in southern and western gardens and are still sold by some specialist nurseries. Unfortunately, susceptible to powdery mildew.

TSARIENSE (Lanata SS)

H4 semi dwarf-low March–April 6b

One of the finest lower-growing species, in and out of flower, and a fairly easy plant to please, its main drawback being its frost-vulnerable expanding flower and growth buds, which makes it a gamble in gardens with frequent spring frosts. Most attractive, pale-pink or white-flushed-pink flowers, spotted crimson, in a truss of 3–5. Superb dark leaves with fawn to rust-coloured indumentum below, whitish

valentinianum

on the new growth. The stems usually have indumentum too. Forms a compact but upright bush which provides attraction all the year round. The dwarfer forms are the most popular. Takes some years to flower, but a very fine foliage plant, and a useful feature in a border of mixed dwarfs. From the district of Tsari in south Tibet. A commonly available clone is **'Yum Yum'** A.M., white flushed pink.

LANATUM is a closely related species usually larger in all parts. The leaves have a thick woolly indumentum and the cream-to-yellow flowers are spotted maroon. Found wild in east Nepal and Sikkim. Grows best in almost pure organic matter.

FLINCKII is another close relation from Bhutan with a thinner more orangy indumentum on both leaf surfaces. Flowers pale yellow, through cream to pink.

VALENTINIANUM (Maddenia SS)

H2–3 dwarf-semi dwarf March–April 7b/8a–7a

An excellent dwarf yellow which unfortunately is tender in most UK gardens. It is very successful in Cornwall, Argyll, and other favourable southern and western areas, but rather a gamble outdoors for us in the east, although we only lose it in severest winters. Bright-yellow flowers, 1–6 per truss, on a usually compact and dense plant with very attractive, fuzzily hairy, button-like leaves and peeling bark. We find it best on tree-stumps here, but in areas of high rainfall it is excellent on mossy rocks and in crevices, imitating the way it grows in its native habitat in Burma and Yunnan. Easy to root, and fairly free-flowering in its best forms, providing that it has plenty of light. A superb foliage plant, and in cold climates well worth some extra protection such as a cloche to protect its opening buds.

MEGERATUM A similar species with smaller hairy leaves and a more compact habit, forming one of the most attractive of all dwarfs out of flower. The flowers vary from creamy to bright yellow, in trusses of 1–3. Rather more difficult to please than the above, and benefits from cloche protection in areas outside the mildest west-coast gardens. The best form available is the Bodnant A.M. form with bright-yellow flowers, quite freely produced.

SULFUREUM Another rather tender yellow-flowered species. Taller and more straggly than the above, with attractive peeling bark. It is worth looking for the deepest-yellow-flowered forms. Hardier forms can be grown outside in moderately cold gardens.

WARDII (Campylocarpa)

H4–(5) low-medium May–June 6b–(6a)

One of the most versatile and popular of the yellow species. No collection is complete without at least one form of this superb plant, named after the great plant hunter F. Kingdon Ward who first collected it. Wide-saucer-shaped flowers of various shades of yellow, with or without a blotch. Smooth rounded leaves on a fairly compact plant which can get leggy in too much shade. A background parent in almost all of the larger yellow hybrids such as 'CREST' and 'HOTEI'. There are many good forms of this species avalable, including 6 A.M. clones awarded over the last 50 years. The best forms for us are from L. & S. 5679 which seems to be particularly hardy (probably H5 [5/6a]), has a bold red blotch and grows later than most, so is less likely to suffer from late frosts. Needs perfect drainage. Forms from this number are quite readily available from UK nurseries, but there are many other fine ones available too.

wardii

wasonii

williamsianum

WASONII (Taliensia SS)

H4–5 low-medium April–May 6b–6a

This very distinct species, from Sichuan Province, China, has fine dark foliage with reddish brown indumentum below. The thinly textured flowers are usually pale yellow but sometimes pink, in loose trusses of 8–15. Freer-flowering from a younger age than most of its relations, hardy throughout the country and best grown in a fairly open situation to retain a compact habit. Rather hard to root and can be hard to obtain.

WILTONII is another distinct Taliense species with unusual rough-textured foliage. White to pink flowers, usually marked and spotted deep pink to crimson. Taller than *wasonii* and also found wild in Sichuan. Quite widely available.

WILLIAMSIANUM (Williamsiana SS)

H4–5 semi dwarf-low April–May 6b–6a

One of the most distinctive of all species, and well worth a place in any garden. Small, neat, smooth, almost round leaves on a bush with a perfect dome-shaped habit if planted in full sun, but which can be a little straggly in too much shade. Pink or occasionally white bell-shaped flowers in small loose trusses of 2–3 or more. Most forms have attractive bronzy young leaves which are alas produced rather early in the spring so are prone to late frosts; avoid planting in a frost pocket. Rare in the wild in Sichuan where it is found on cliffs. Named after the Williams family of great Cornish gardeners. Has been very widely used as a parent, passing on its excellent characteristics to such hybrids as 'LINDA', 'MOONSTONE', 'BOW BELLS' and 'WHISPERINGROSE'. Easily rooted and widely available.

yakushimanum 'Koichiro Wada' F.C.C.

YAKUSHIMANUM (Pontica SS)

H5 semi-dwarf–low late May-early June 5/6a

One of the best-known and most popular of all species, and the most popular parent of all for hybridizing. Flowers open pale pink and fade quickly to white, in dense full trusses in the better forms. Famous for its excellent foliage, it has convex leaves with thick indumentum below, and usually silvery above on the new growth. Most forms are compact, producing a slow-growing dense mound. Best in an open site, as the shape is spoiled in shade, although it usually grows there quite happily. Free-flowering, and very hardy; suitable for any UK garden. Always in great demand and as it is rather hard to root the many selected clones are often grafted. Good from seed if the best forms are used as parents. The F.C.C. form **'Koichiro Wada'** is one of the best clones, but many others are very similar. Native to Yakushima island in Japan, and introduced into the UK in 1934. Its many hybrids known as 'yak' hybrids feature prominently in the hybrid section of this book. They are characterized by being hardy, low-growing, free-flowering plants with fine foliage, suitable for the

degronianum

small garden. Some of the best include: 'DOPEY', 'TITIAN BEAUTY', 'KEN JANECK' and 'SEVEN STARS'. Several related Japanese species are also available:

MAKINOI is closely related with narrower leaves, giving a dense spiky effect. Not as easy to grow as the above, and perhaps best as a grafted plant.

DEGRONIANUM is similar to *yakushimanum* but not as striking in foliage. The flowers are usually pale pink. A good clone is **'Gerald Loder'** A.M.

DEGRONIANUM var. HEPTAMERUM is the new name for *metternichii*. Another variation on the same theme. Flowers usually pink. Leaves similar to *yakushimanum*, but variable in habit ranging from compact to rather open.

YUNNANENSE (Triflora SS)

H3–4 medium-tall May 7a–6b

One of the best and most floriferous of the Triflora SS. Relatively small leaves and flowers on a fairly vigorous, easily grown plant, inclined to be rather straggly. Flowers white to pink with olive-to-crimson spots, often from buds in the top leaf axils as well as the terminal bud so producing a mass of flower, from a young plant onwards. A very variable species of wide distribution in the wild, coming from several Chinese provinces in addition to Yunnan which it is named after. Also comes from a wide altitudinal range resulting in a variation in hardiness, the more tender forms being

yunnanense ►

oreotrephes

very susceptible to bark split from spring frosts. Best in a fairly sunny situation to avoid straggliness, and sometimes benefits from pruning. Some forms are nearly deciduous and most have reddish leaves in winter. Eventually this species and its relations can grow into bushes at least 10ft (3m) high, so give plenty of room. Roots quite easily and many good clones are commercially available.

DAVIDSONIANUM Closely related to the above. Best clones have pink flowers, with or without spotting. Only selected clones should be accepted. The F.C.C. clone has fine rich-pink flowers, but is somewhat tender at Glendoick. Other good, somewhat hardier clones also exist.

RIGIDUM Also very closely related with smaller, more glaucous, stiffer leaves on a generally more rigid, less vigorous plant. Usually available in its white forms, but can also be pink, purple and lilac.

OREOTREPHES H4 (6b). Another fine Triflora species, which is hardier than most members of the section, so can be planted more widely than the above. Flowers in many shades of pink, purple and off-white, on an upright but tidy grower, more compact than the above, with fine glaucous leaves on most forms.

HYBRIDS

'A. BEDFORD'
(mauve seedling X *ponticum*)

H4–5 tall late May–June 6b–6a

This popular hybrid is named after Arthur Bedford who was a head gardener at Exbury. Pyramidal trusses of 11–16 flowers, lavender-mauve with a deep brownish red flare. Easily grown, vigorous and upright, perhaps best as a background plant. Distinctive thick foliage with shiny leaves on purple leaf stalks. Fairly easy to root, readily available, and probably hardy enough for any UK garden. F.C.C.T. 1958.

'A. Bedford' F.C.C.T.

'Alison Johnstone' A.M.

'ALISON JOHNSTONE'
(*yunnanense* X *cinnabarinum* ssp. *xanthocodon* Concatenans)

H4 low-medium May 6b

A widely grown hybrid for favourable areas with golden amber flowers, flushed pink, fading from apricot, in trusses of 9–10. Fine foliage shows influence of CINNABARINUM with rounded bluish-green leaves and a dense compact habit close to that of Concatenans. We find this plant hardy, free-flowering and reliable, budding up at 3–4 years and easy to root. Although it probably flowers best in full sun, we find that the foliage is best in a little shade and shelter. In full exposure, the leaves tend to develop a yellow edging. Not as susceptible to mildew as some of its relatives. Recommended and widely available. A.M. 1945.

'BISKRA' H4–5 (6b–5) is the hardiest of the CINNABARINUM type hybrids, and suitable for the severest areas of the UK in a sheltered site. Pendant bell-shaped vermilion and biscuit-coloured flowers in loose trusses on an upright slender bush. Not everyone's colour, but very useful for its hardiness. A.M. 1940. Susceptible to powdery mildew.

'PEACE' H3–4 (7a–6b) Less hardy than the above, but similar in appearance and habit. Pendulous white flowers providing a fine contrast to other CINNABARINUM species and hybrids. A.M.T. 1946. Susceptible to powdery mildew.

'ANNA BALDSIEFEN'
('Pioneer' selfed)

H4 semi dwarf-low late March–April 6b

A fine low-growing American hybrid which we introduced to the UK. Racemes of vibrant phlox-pink, star-shaped flowers with deeper-coloured edges. It has a compact pillar-like upright habit, is extremely free-flowering in Scotland, is easy to root and has fine bronzy-red winter colour. Susceptible to rust fungus. One of the brightest-pink dwarf hybrids, hardy enough for most parts of the country, but rather early-flowering, so not for frost pockets. A.M.T. 1979.

'ANNA ROSE WHITNEY'
(*griersonianum* X 'Countess of Derby')

H5 tall May–June 6b/6a

This American hybrid has large flowers of deep rose-pink with some brown spotting, in somewhat open trusses of 12–21. Foliage is large, thick and matt-green. Hardy, easy to grow, but very vigorous, needing plenty of room, and benefitting from occasional pinching and pruning. Rather susceptible to powdery mildew, and for this reason, and for the best habit, we suggest an open planting site. On the whole, it is quite free-flowering but we find that it does not bud up too well as a young plant. Becoming popular and widely available. A.M.T. 1987.

'ARCTIC TERN'
(*trichostomum* X *Ledum* species)?

H5 low May–June 5/6a

This fine and unusual plant has ledum-like, 20-flower crowded trusses of white, slightly green in the throat. Hardy, vigorous, easy and buds up young. Needs full sun to keep it compact. The leaves are small on a normally airy but tidy plant. An improvement on Ledum species for winter foliage, as 'Arctic Tern's leaves remain green and healthy looking in winter. Roots easily and is becoming more widely available. Very hardy, and later-flowering than most dwarfs, so it should avoid most spring frosts in high altitude and severe gardens. A.M.T. 1984.

'Arctic Tern' A.M.T.

'Bashful'

'AZOR' g.
(*griersonianum* X *fortunei* ssp. *discolor*)

H(3)–4 tall late June–early July (7a)–6b

One of the most popular late-flowering hybrids. Loose trusses of salmon-pink flowers on a very straggly often sparse bush with long leaves. Inclined to have poor foliage. There are several forms of this around; unfortunately the best ones are seldom seen in commerce. Only really of merit because of its late flowering. Needs some shelter, and not for the coldest gardens. Somewhat susceptible to powdery mildew. Free-flowering, easy to root and widely available. A.M. 1933.

'BAGSHOT RUBY'
(thomsonii X)

H5 medium May 5/6a

An old but still popular red hybrid which is hardly enough for any UK garden. Conical trusses of ruby-red flowers with contrasting white stamens. Dull, dark-green foliage, on a fairly dense, upright plant. Quite good, but not as spectacular as the larger-flowered red hardy hybrids from Holland and the USA. A.M. 1916.

'BASHFUL' cl.
(*yakushimanum* X 'Doncaster')

H5 low May 6a

One of the seven Dwarf 'yak' hybrids from Waterers. One of the tallest and least dense of the group. Flowers open camellia-rose, with a large blotch of reddish brown, fading to off-white. Leaves long and thin with red stems, no indumentum but somewhat silvery new growth. Not particularly attractive or spectacular, but reliable and one of the hardiest 'yak' hybrids. Fairly easy to root, buds up young but not always one of the most floriferous. Widely available.

'Blue Diamond' F.C.C.

'DOC' is another of the seven Dwarfs, one of the hardiest of the group. Smallish compact trusses of light-pink-frilled flowers, which are not long-lasting. The foliage is rather nondescript and overall one of the least exciting 'yak' hybrids. H.C. 1978.

'PINK CHERUB' is rose pink with a paler centre. Rather ordinary. F.C.C.T. 1968.

'VINTAGE ROSÉ' has large rose-pink flowers which fade to near-white. Fine dark foliage with thick indumentum below. H.C. 1979.

'BLUE DIAMOND' g.
('Intrifast' X *augustinii*)

H4–5 low April–May 6b–6a

Still the most popular of the lepidote blues but likely to be gradually replaced by some of the new German hybrids. Clusters of violet-blue flowers on a dense upright grower, eventually reaching 5–6ft (1.5–1.8m). Best in full sun. Easy to root and readily available. There are several different clones about; the F.C.C. clone has the best flowers although it sometimes suffers from leaf spot and chlorosis, as do some of the other clones. F.C.C. 1939.

'BLUE TIT' *g.* was one of the first of the dwarf 'blues' to be raised, and still very popular. Grey-blue flowers on a fairly compact plant which often has horrible yellow and spotted foliage. We feel that this has been superseded but it is still widely available. A clone known as **'Magor'** which we obtained in West Germany is the best clone we have seen.

'Blue Peter' F.C.C.T.

'SAINT BREWARD'
'SAINT TUDY' are two virtually indistinguishable hybrids with very fine large bright violet-blue flowers. Not free-flowering as young plants, and they tend to have poor winter foliage, but the flowers are very fine and they make a good substitute for *AUGUSTINII* in smaller gardens. In the very coldest gardens, we would recommend the hardier 'GRISTEDE', 'AZURWOLKE', and 'SACKO'. F.C.C. (both).

'BLUE PETER'
(*ponticum* hybrid?)

H5 medium May 5/6a

The best known larger 'blue' flowered hybrid. Very frilly pale lavender-blue flowers, with a purple flare, in a tight conical truss of around 15. Leaves glossy, tending to bend down at the edges. Although well-branched, the habit is rather sprawly. Easy to root, vigorous and buds up young. Readily available. F.C.C.T. 1958.

'BLUE ENSIGN' is virtually identical in flower, less sprawling in habit but sometimes suffers leaf spot. Becoming better known. A.M. 1959.

'BOW BELLS' g.
('Corona' X *williamsianum*)

H4 low-medium early May 6b

One of the oldest *WILLIAMSIANUM* hybrids, and still very popular. Light-pink cup-shaped flowers in lax trusses. Upright-growing but quite tidy, with rounded leaves, bronzy when young. Needs sun to avoid straggliness. There are several clones around, and the ones we have tried are not particularly easy to please, suffering from yellowing of the leaves. Others may be better. Although 'BOW BELLS' is quite good, we prefer some of the hardier and easier European *WILLIAMSIANUM* hybrids such as 'LINDA' and 'GARTENDIREKTOR GLOCKER', and the more compact 'PINK PEBBLE'. A.M. 1935.

'BRIGITTE'
('*insigne* x 'Mrs J. G. Millais')

H5 low-medium June 5/6a

Attractive and unusual rose flowers paling to white towards the centre, with an olive-green flare, 19–23 in a full truss. Pointed, shiny leaves on a fairly compact plant. The best *INSIGNE* hybrid that we have seen. Newly commercially available.

'BRITANNIA'
('Queen Wilhelmina' X 'Stanley Davies')

H4–5 low-medium late May–June 6b–6a

One of the most widely grown large-flowered red hybrids. Its popularity is surprising, since it is hard to root, shy flowering until 4–5 years of age, and has rather dull yellow-green foliage especially in full sun, and the shade of red is not very striking. What merit does it have then? It has large bright-scarlet flowers in full trusses and is a compact spreading grower, not nearly as tall and vigorous as the 'Pink Pearl' types. It has now been superseded and should be grown less, but it is still widely available. F.C.C.T. 1937.

'CARITA' g.
('Naomi' X *campylocarpum*)

H3–4 medium April–May 7a–6b

Several different-coloured clones of this Exbury cross were named. Flat-topped trusses of pink-yellow flowers. Slow to bud up when young. Habit is quite good, but can be open when old. Foliage is rounded and shiny and inclined to burn in hot sun, so best in light shade. Most clones are fair to

'Brigitte'

root. The following are selected clones: **'A.M.' 1945** has trusses of 10–12 pale primrose-yellow flowers. **'Inchmery'** is rose/salmon pink, and biscuit-yellow, fading to near-white—this is the pinkest clone. **'Golden Dream'** is golden yellow, fading to cream. The deepest-yellow clone taller and later than 'A.M.' Probably the best clone.

'CARMEN' g.
(*sanguineum* ssp. *didymum* X *forrestii* Repens)

H4 dwarf-semi dwarf April–May 6b

For some reason no clone of this extremely popular dwarf red was ever selected, and there are several different ones in commerce. Waxy dark-red flowers with paler stamens in flat trusses cover small dark leaves on a dense bush, wider than tall. Very easy to root, and free-flowering from 3–4 years of age. It needs good drainage and likes to have cool roots and a little shade to prevent it becoming chlorotic and sparse. Not for the coldest gardens and difficult in areas of high rainfall, but at its best a very impressive dwarf. Readily available.

'CHARMAINE' ('Charm' x 'May Day')? Much brighter red flowers than the above and the leaves have a good brown indumentum below. Similar habit to 'Carmen'. Not for gardens colder than Glendoick, as it sometimes suffers barksplit. A.M. 1946.

'CHIKOR'
(*rupicola* var. *chryseum* X *ludlowii*)

H4 dwarf May 6b

Our first successful hybrid and a highly rated plant in many areas. Named after an Asian bird which resembles a partridge. Soft-yellow, flat-faced flowers with deeper yellow spots, 3 to 6 per truss. Tiny slightly shiny leaves on a twiggy compact rounded little bush. Bronzy winter foliage. Must have loose, well drained soil and a cool root run and does not like excessive summer heat. Good for bonsai. Widely available. F.C.C.T. 1968.

'GOLDILOCKS' (*xanthostephanum* x *rupicola* var. *chryseum*) Small deep-yellow flowers on a fairly upright but neat plant with dark foliage. Distinctive, and with the deepest yellow flowers available on any dwarf hybrid. Not for areas colder than Glendoick, as it is rather bud-tender. Becoming available.

'CHIONOIDES'
(*ponticum* hybrid)

H5 low-medium late May–June 5

One of the most reliable hardy hybrids for general use. Pink-tinged buds open to clear white flowers with a yellow flare in small compact trusses. Rather narrow leaves on a dense bush of moderate growth about as wide as high, capable of standing full exposure. Propagates well, buds up young, and usually reliable and easy. Despite its rather small flowers, this is an attractive hybrid, with an excellent dense habit and a rugged constitution. Readily available.

'MADAME MASSON' is very similar to the above. Larger flowers than 'Chionoides' on a earlier-flowering, slightly taller plant. Buds young, very hardy, and good as a windbreak.

'Christmas Cheer'

'CHRISTMAS CHEER'
(*caucasicum* hybrid)

H5 low-medium February–April 5/6a

A very popular, medium-sized early hybrid. Blush-pink flowers with deeper stripes, fading to almost white, in small tight trusses. The flowers open over a long period during mild winters with a final flush in April. Leaves medium-green with thin, smooth, brown indumentum below. Very bud-hardy, free-flowering from 2–3 years and easily rooted. Easy to grow and usually sun-tolerant though foliage may discolour. Probably the most reliable and easy of the early-flowering hybrids, and suitable for anywhere in Britain.

'CILPINENSE'
(*ciliatum* X *moupinense*)

H3–4 semi-dwarf February–March 7a–6b

One of the most popular early-flowering hybrids. Flowers pale blush-pink touched deeper, with darker anthers, in trusses of 2–3. Shiny bright-green hairy leaves on a fairly compact mound-like plant. Exceptionally free-flowering; when at its best not a leaf can be seen. Roots well and very easy to grow. Buds vulnerable to frost once they swell so protection is desirable, and not worth growing in inland or high altitude gardens with no prospect of frost-free periods in early spring. Widely available. F.C.C. 1968.

'Crest' F.C.C.

'SNOW LADY' is a similar American hybrid with pure-white flowers. Slower-growing than 'Cilpinense', and with more attractive hairy leaves.

'CREAMY CHIFFON'
(unknown)

H4? low May 6b?

One of the few rhododendrons with double flowers. Salmon orange buds open to small trusses of gardenia-like creamy yellow flowers. Habit is compact and dense, and it has rather characterless smooth rounded leaves. Recently introduced into the UK and will probably become widely available.

◄ 'Snow Lady'

'QUEEN ANNE'S' is another new American hybrid with double white flowers. Very hardy and taller than the above.

'CREST'
(*wardii* X 'Lady Bessborough')

H4 tall May 6b

For a long time considered the best yellow larger hybrid, and for sheer perfection of flower and truss it still has few equals. Orangy buds open to heavily-textured long-lasting clear primrose-yellow flowers, slightly darker in the centre, in a full, elegant truss of about 12. Deep-green shiny leaves. The habit is upright and tree-like with ascending open branches. Fairly hard to root. A little tender when young, and

'Curlew' F.C.C.T.

takes some years to bud up but quite free-flowering when mature. Does best in open woodland. Not for the coldest gardens. Widely available. F.C.C. 1953.

'CUNNINGHAM'S WHITE'
(*caucasicum* x *ponticum* Album)

H5 low-medium May–June 5

A very old hybrid raised in Edinburgh. Mauve buds open to white flowers with yellow-green-brown markings. The clone we grow has an upright truss of about 20 flowers. Another clone, more commonly grown in mainland Europe, has a less impressive loose truss of about 8 flowers. A dense spreading grower, usually quite compact. Buds up at 4–5 years and is very easy to root. This old hybrid is renowned for its tremendous adaptability. It is pollution-tolerant, grows well in neutral or even slightly alkaline soil and is useful as a windbreak, hedge or background plant where PONTICUM is too invasive. Popular as an understock for grafting. Widely available.

'CURLEW'
(*ludlowii* x *fletcherianum*)

H4 dwarf late April–May 6b

One of our series of 'bird' hybrids. It is a miracle that two of the most temperamental dwarf species have produced such fine offspring. Flowers carried in trusses of one to three, bright-yellow with deeper shading and greenish-brown spotting. Flowers are relatively large for the small deep-green leaves. Can look a little sparse in less-than-ideal conditions and does best in a clump. Can be rather bud-tender, but usually its bright showy flowers completely hide the foliage, giving one of the finest displays of any dwarf. Easy to root, buds up young and a good doer. Readily available. F.C.C. 1969, F.C.C.T. 1986.

'EUAN COX' (*ludlowii* x *hanceanum* Nanum), raised at Glendoick, is a later-flowering deep-yellow which is equally floriferous. Very compact, smaller in all parts and slower growing. A.M.T. 1981.

'CYNTHIA'
(*catawbiense* hybrid)

H5 tall late May–June 5

This is one of the most popular old hardy hybrids, nearly as well-known as 'Pink Pearl'. Large pyramidal trusses of up to 24 flowers of deep rose-pink with extensive deeper-crimson staining. There is a lot of magenta in the flower, but it is not harsh and its darker staining sets off the colour well. Easy to root, buds up young and grows into huge upright bush, too big for the small garden. One of the most reliable old hybrids, hardy enough for any UK garden. Very widely available.

'DAVID'
('Hugh Koster' x *neriiflorum*)??

H4 tall late April–May 6b

Impressive, brilliant blood-red flowers with frilly margins, in rounded trusses of 16–19, deeply spotted within. A bright pure red and earlier than most similar hybrids. Unusual vertical growing habit, forming an upright bush. Fairly easy to root and buds up young. Needs some degree of protection from wind and frost but has survived recent hard winters at Glendoick. Widely available. A.M.T. 1957.

'DOPEY'
([*facetum* x 'Fabia'] x [*yakushimanum* x 'Fabia Tangerine'])??

H4 low-medium May–June 6b

One of Waterer's 'yak' hybrid Seven Dwarfs. This excellent hybrid is only one-quarter YAKUSHIMANUM but the latter's influence is seen in the habit and flowers but without the fading out seen in the first generation 'yak' hybrids. Deep, glossy-red, long-lasting flowers which bleach a little towards the margins, with dark brown spots, in a full truss of around 16. Medium dull-green leaves with no indumentum, but with a silvery dusting on the new growth, on a compact but fairly upright plant. Buds young and easy to root. Becoming popular and widely available. F.C.C.T. 1979.

'Dopey' F.C.C.T.

'Dora Amateis' F.C.C.T.

'DORA AMATEIS'
(*minus* Carolinianum x *ciliatum*)

H5 semi-dwarf April–May 5

This is one of the most widely grown dwarf lepidote hybrids to come from the USA and probably the most attractive Carolinianum hybrid yet raised. Very pale-pink buds open pure white, with pink markings and small green flecks, in a lax truss of 6–8. Usually a compact grower with long, palish green leaves, turned down at the edges. Extremely free-flowering, hardy and reliable, and reasonably hardy in the swelling bud. Quite easily rooted, and easy to grow, best in full sun. Occasionally suffers from yellowish foliage. Widely available. F.C.C.T. 1981.

'EGRET'
(*campylogynum* white x *racemosum* 'White Lace')

H4 dwarf May 6b

Raised at Glendoick, this very distinctive new dwarf has tiny white bells on long flower stalks, giving an effect somewhat reminiscent of white heather. Very clean, small, shiny, mid-green leaves on a compact, neat plant, wider than high. Easy to root, very easily grown, best in sun for free flowering. Probably not hardy enough for severest gardens. Becoming popular. A.M.T. 1987.

'Egret' A.M.T.

'ELIZABETH'
(*forrestii* Repens x *griersonianum*)

H4 low April–May 6b

This hybrid is so well known that it hardly needs describing, having become the most popular semi-dwarf ever raised. Masses of bright-red, open-mouthed, funnel-shaped flowers, 6–9 per truss. Medium-green, slightly rough leaves on a rounded, compact plant. Very easy to root and to grow and buds up young. Good in sun or some shade. May open some flowers in autumn. At its best, it is so free-flowering that it hides its foliage and can make a startling informal hedge. Unfortunately it is very prone to powdery mildew, requiring regular fungicide spraying. Hardy enough for all but the coldest gardens, but late growth sometimes vulnerable to early autumn frosts. Very widely available. The German hybrids 'SCARLET WONDER', 'ELISABETH HOBBIE' etc. are hardier and more disease-resistant substitutes, but have smaller flowers. F.C.C. 1943.

'Elizabeth Lockhart' H.C.T.

'CREEPING JENNY' from the same cross has similar but slightly smaller flowers. The chief difference is its lower-growing habit, tending to creep with some branches growing outwards and downwards. Forms a mound in shade but grows more flat in sun. Seems to be considerably more resistant to powdery mildew than 'Elizabeth'.

◄ 'Creeping Jenny'

'ELIZABETH LOCKHART'
(sport of 'Hummingbird')

H4 semi-dwarf April–May 6b

This hybrid is a sport or mutation which adds a new dimension to rhododendron foliage. Leaves rounded, very shiny and a deep maroon-purple when young, only slightly less vivid with age, on a compact, rounded bush, wider than high. Unfortunately the foliage may partially or completely revert, especially in a sunny site, and it seems to perform best in light shade, especially in the south where the sun is stronger. Pruning out reverted shoots is advised, but faded ones may still produce purple new growth. The loose cherry-red bell-shaped flowers are smaller and deeper-coloured than those of the 'HUMMINGBIRD' clones that we have seen. Prone to bark-split, and not for coldest gardens. Roots easily and quite widely available. H.C.T. 1972.

'Fabia' A.M.

'FABIA' g.
(dichroanthum X griersonianum)

H3–4 low-medium late
May–June 7a–6b

A variable hybrid, the cross having been made several times. All clones have loose 7–10-flower trusses of salmon, orange and red shades. The leaves are medium dark-green with light indumentum. Stays compact in full sun but needs some shade in most areas. Can become rather loose and floppy, as branches are rather thin. Easy to root, buds up young and flowers are relatively long-lasting. One of the most popular of the 'orange' hybrids. The most readily available clones are: **'A.M.'** 1934, scarlet flowers, shaded orange; **'Tangerine'** A.M. 1940, soft vermilion with pinker shading at edge; **'Waterer'**, salmon-pink with orange; **'Roman Pottery'**, pale orange with coppery edges.

'MEDUSA' This has loose trusses of orange, red tinged flowers, that are amongst the nearest to true orange available. Easy to grow, and unusual, but like 'Fabia', not for the coldest gardens. 'SONATA' is a hardier alternative.

'Fastuosum Flore Pleno'

'FASTUOSUM FLORE PLENO'
(*catawbiense* X *ponticum*)

H5 tall June 5

This very old hybrid is well-known for its unusual, semi-double, pale bluish-mauve flowers, with a small greenish-brown flare, held in loose but large trusses. Dark, dull, convex leaves on an upright but fairly dense and compact bush. Roots easily, free-flowering, buds up young and the flowers are long-lasting, especially in some shade. Rugged, versatile, sun- and wind-tolerant and suitable for any UK garden. Useful for its late flowering. Very widely available.

'FRAGRANTISSIMUM'
(*edgeworthii* X *formosum*)

H2 medium May–June 7b/8a

This is by far the best-known of the many tender MADDENIA hybrids. Usually grown in a greenhouse or conservatory, except in mild gardens where it can be grown outside. Funnel-shaped flowers are white tinged pink, with a yellow throat in trusses of 2–4. It has a strong fragrance, sometimes described as being like nutmeg. The rough narrow leaves are scaly and hairy. It is famous for its deplorably straggly arching habit and looks best on a wall, or trained around stakes. F.C.C. 1868.

'Lady Alice Fitzwilliam' F.C.C.

'LADY ALICE FITZWILLIAM' is more compact and hardier but has a less powerful scent. Good outside in the south and west, and can be grown in very sheltered sites, such as on a wall, in eastern districts. We can grow it outside at Glendoick, but it loses flower buds in harder-than-average winters. F.C.C. 1881.

'HARRY TAGG' is a more compact, spreading hybrid worth growing outdoors in a very sheltered site even in gardens as severe as our own. White flowers tinged pink, with a yellow throat. Very free-flowering. A.M. 1958.

'FURNIVALL'S DAUGHTER' (seedling of 'Mrs Furnival'?)

H4–5 medium May–June 6b–6a

A very showy seedling of 'Mrs Furnival'. Bright-pink flowers with a larger, strawberry-red flare in a full conical truss of about 15. Rounded, rough foliage, yellowish to deep green on an upright rounded plant, often wider than high. Fastidious as to soil conditions, sometimes producing a miserable root system and chlorotic foliage. Free-flowering from 3–4 years old. Very popular. F.C.C.T. 1961.

'MRS FURNIVAL' has a smaller truss and smaller leaves, is slower-growing and harder to root. Better foliage than the above. Light rose-pink flowers with a bold sienna flare. Still popular. F.C.C.T. 1948.

'Mrs Furnival' F.C.C.T. ➤

'Mrs G. W. Leak' F.C.C.T.

'Ginny Gee' S.P.A.

'MRS G. W. LEAK' has very striking light rose-pink flowers with a large heavy brown and crimson flare in an upright conical truss. Does not bud up well as a young plant but is free-flowering thereafter. Less hardy than the above. More vigorous than 'Mrs Furnival' but the dull-olive green foliage often suffers leaf-spotting after the winter. Still popular and widely available. F.C.C.T. 1948.

'GINNY GEE'

(*keiskei* 'Yaku Fairy' x *racemosum* F. 19404)

H5 dwarf late April–May 5/6a

One of the finest dwarf hybrids ever raised and sure to become one of the most popular. Bright-pink buds open to light blush-pink flowers, fading to white tinged pink giving a two-tone effect, in multiple trusses forming a sheet of bloom that hides the foliage. Healthy leaves on a compact twiggy plant, growing wider than high. Easy to root and tougher than most dwarfs, although its flowers are vulnerable to frosts. Buds up very young and succeeds in sun or some shade. Becoming widely available. S.P.A. 1985.

'GOLDEN STAR'

(*fortunei* X *wardii*)

H4–5 medium-tall May 6b–5/6a

An American hybrid which we at Glendoick introduced to the UK. Pinky-cream buds open to pale mimosa-yellow flowers in almost full trusses of about 7. Free-flowering, fair to root and has healthy, shiny, rounded foliage. Easy to grow, buds up at 4–5 years and is one of the best yellows for general planting, being hardy, vigorous, easy to please and suitable for most gardens. Should become more popular.

'Golden Torch' A.M.

'GOLDEN TORCH' (*yakushimanum* hybrid)

H4 low May–early June 6b

The most popular of the UK-raised yellow 'yak' hybrids. Salmon-pink buds open to compact trusses of soft yellow, quickly fading to cream, faintly spotted deeper. A disappointing colour for its name, being closer to ivory than to yellow. Compact and dense with lightly indumented leaves. Easy to root, buds up young and now readily available. A.M. 1984. There has long been a shortage of low-growing yellows suitable for general planting. The following hybrids include some new ones which seem promising:

'FLAVA' (H5, 5) is a German YAKUSHIMANUM hybrid with deeper-yellow flowers than the above. Several clones exist, but most have tight trusses of light-yellow flowers with a small reddish blotch in the centre. Deep-green leaves with no indumentum.

'MARIETTA' (H5, 5) is another similar hybrid from Germany. Fairly full trusses of pale, clear yellow, very frilly flowers. This and 'Flava' have been recently introduced into commerce in the UK.

'BUTTERMINT' has flat trusses of light yellow with pink shading. A neat, compact, free-flowering, newly introduced hybrid which seems promising.

'CANARY' Bright lemon-yellow flowers, produced in April. Flowers sometimes open poorly, and foliage is rather yellowish, but one of the hardiest low yellow hybrids, and quite widely available.

'GOLDEN WITT' is a new American hybrid with small but full trusses of quite deep-yellow flowers with red spotting. A low-growing, fairly hardy hybrid which will probably become popular.

'Taurus'

'GOLDSWORTH ORANGE'
(*dichroanthum* X *fortunei*)

H4–(5) medium June 6b(5/6a)

One of the most popular orange hybrids, although the epithet 'orange' is a bit far-fetched—the flowers are salmon-pink with orange tones, spotted brown, in loose, flat trusses of about 10. An upright but dense compact bush, not too vigorous, with deep-green leaves on distinctive red leaf stalks. Rather slow to bud up as a young plant and fairly easy to root. Flowers last best in some shade. Widely available. A.M. 1959.

'GOMER WATERER'
(*catawbiense* hybrid containing *griffithianum*)

H5 medium early June 5

One of the most outstanding and versatile of hardy hybrids for severe climates, and well worth growing in milder areas too. Rosy-lilac buds open to white flowers flushed mauve-pink at the edges, with a large yellowish-brown flare, in trusses of up to 20. Leathery, dark green, healthy leaves on a vigorous, dense compact plant. Sun- and wind-resistant, buds up young and easy to root. Widely available and highly recommended. A.M. 1906.

'GRACE SEABROOK'
('Jean Marie de Montague' x *strigillosum*?)

H4 medium April–early May 6b

This is undoubtedly one of the best red American-raised hybrids, very attractive in or out of flower. Flowers are currant-red at margins, shading to blood-red at the centre, in a full tight truss of 10–15. Leaves are large, pointed, very thick and deep green, on a vigorous plant which needs room to spread. Buds up at 4–5 years of age, sometimes earlier. It may be too early flowering for frost pockets but the plant is otherwise fairly rugged. Sure to become very popular.

'TAURUS' is from the same cross. Similar, with the added bonus of having red winter buds instead of green, but slightly slower to bud up as a young plant. Probably hardier than 'GRACE SEABROOK'.

ETTA BURROWS' ('Fusilier' x *strigillosum*) H3–4 (7a–6b). Fine bright blood-red flowers and long, narrow, rather pale, STRIGILLOSUM-like, convex leaves. Not for coldest gardens, and flowering in April, it may have its flowers frosted.

'GRISTEDE'
(?*impeditum* hybrid)

H5 low April 5/6a

Another 'blue' of the 'BLUE DIAMOND' type, raised in Germany. Funnel-shaped violet-blue flowers in clusters. We find that although the flowers are not as good as those of the best form of 'Blue Diamond', it is hardier and the leaves remain a healthier green during the winter. Easy to root.

'AZURWOLKE' has rounded clusters of fine medium violet-blue flowers on a more open bush with larger leaves.

'PENHEALE BLUE' Bright violet-blue flowers on a vigorous, upright plant with healthy foliage which turns reddish and bronzy in winter. Taller than the above hybrids. Promising and becoming quite popular. F.C.C.T. 1981.

'GRUMPY'
(*yakushimanum* x unnamed hybrid)

H4–5 semi dwarf-low May–June 6b–5/6a

One of the Seven Dwarfs 'yak' hybrids. Orange buds open to creamy flowers with rose edging and orange spotting. When the flowers first open, the pastel shade combination is unusual and attractive, but the flowers soon fade out to a pale cream. A dense, compact, spreading bush with indumentum on the lower leaf surface. Easily rooted and buds up well in full sun, but perhaps would hold its subtle colouring better in some shade. One of the best 'yak' hybrids for foliage. Becoming widely available. A.M.T. 1979.

'HARVEST MOON'
('Mrs Lindsay Smith' x *campylocarpum* hybrid)

H4–5 low-medium May 6b–6a

Full rounded trusses of pale lemon-yellow flowers fading to cream, with a small red/brown flare. Rounded foliage is heavily veined and tends to be yellowish, especially on the new growth. A fairly compact spreading grower which is attractive in flower and widely available but which may become less popular as deeper-coloured hardy yellows become more widely distributed. A.M.T. 1948.

'HELENE SCHIFFNER'
(*arboreum* hybrid)

H4–5 low May–June 6b–6a

Mauve buds open to full tight trusses of pure white with very faint brown markings. Stiff pointed leaves, almost black buds and a red leaf stalk on a compact, slow-growing plant. Easy to root and buds up young. One of the hardiest pure-white hybrids. Raised in Dresden in East Germany late last century. Fairly readily available. F.C.C. 1893.

'Hoppy'

'HOPPY'
([*yakushimanum* X 'Doncaster'??] selfed)

H5 low May–early June 5/6a

Very frilled lilac-pink flowers which fade to white, in fine trusses. Convex leaves with no indumentum, on a medium grower. One of the best 'yak' hybrids we have seen in this colour, spectacular in full flower and very hardy. Widely available. A.M. 1977

'SLEEPY' is a similar sister seedling with larger leaves and a less compact habit. Widely available.

'CAROLINE ALLBROOK' Has darker lavender-purple flowers which fade to off-white. More dwarf and compact than the above, free-flowering and good if you like the colour. A.M. 1977.

'CENTENNIAL CELEBRATION' Frilly pale lavender-pink flowers. New growth silvery. Named for the centenary of Washington State, USA.

'MORNING CLOUD' Almost white flowers, with slight flushing of lavender-pink. Leaves have creamy buff indumentum below. Very free-flowering. A.M. 1971.

'HOTEI'
('Goldsworth Orange' x [*souliei* x *wardii*])

H4 medium May 6b

Named after a Japanese God, this has some of the deepest yellow-coloured flowers of any rhododendron. Aureolin-yellow flowers, 10–12 per truss, of good substance, with deeper shading and a prominent calyx. Leaves are smallish and a medium green on a dense grower. Generally free-flowering from about 6 years. It sometimes over-flowers, bending down its branches, and it tends to hang onto its spent flowers. Somewhat prone to mildew and inclined to defoliate during shipping. Needs a sheltered position and very good drainage, and not hardy enough for the coldest gardens. It is worth extra care to please. Quite widely available. A.M. 1974.

'HUMMING BIRD' g.
(*haematodes* X *williamsianum*)

H(3)–4 semi-dwarf April–May (7a)–6b

Cherry-red to rose, bell-shaped flowers of good substance in a very lax truss of 4 or more. Good dark rounded foliage with slight indumentum, on a compact mound-shaped plant in the better forms. Roots and grows easily. There are many forms of this about and it is important to obtain a good one as some clones are tender and have poor flowers. Sometimes a little slow to bud up. Susceptible to bark-split and not for the coldest gardens. For foliage effect, both of the parents would be preferable. Widely available.

'Hotei' A.M.

'St Merryn' F.C.C.T.

'HYDON DAWN'
(*yakushimanum* x 'Springbok')

H5 low May–early June 5

Attractive, frilled, pale-pink flowers, blotched deeper in the centre, fading to white, in a rounded truss of 14–18. The fairly dark, glossy foliage has a covering of cream indumentum on a very compact plant. Free-flowering from about 3 years, easy to please, and should be hardy in any UK garden. Becoming widely available. A.M.T. 1986.

'HYDON HUNTER' is a sister seedling with cherry-red flowers, paler in the centre, which holds its colour quite well. Dark-green long leaves on a tall rather lanky plant. Not particularly good. F.C.C.T. 1979.

'RENOIR' has pale-pink flowers with contrasting strong red spotting in the throat. Not the best foliage or habit, but the flowers are showy. A.M. 1961.

'INTRIFAST'
(*intricatum* X *fastigiatum*)

H5 dwarf April–May 5/6a

Very similar to a good form of FASTIGIATUM, with clusters of small, violet-blue flowers. Extremely dense and compact, with fine glaucous-blue foliage, possibly better than either parent. Free-flowering, easily grown, best in full sun. Hardy in any UK garden. Quite widely available.

'ST MERRYN' is another very compact hybrid, with deep purple-blue flowers. Amongst the finest flowers of all the dwarf 'blues' but not always the easiest plant to please. Recommended. Fairly widely available. F.C.C.T. 1986.

'JEAN MARIE DE MONTAGUE'
(syn. 'The Hon. Jean Marie de Montague')
(*griffithianum* hybrid)

H4 medium early-mid May 6b

One of the many popular Dutch hybrids, this is the most common red hybrid in western USA, but is not quite so widely grown in the U.K. Rounded trusses of 10–14 crimson-scarlet flowers on a compact, rather slow-growing plant which can become rather sparse as it gets older. Fine thick leaves on a healthy, easily grown plant, suitable for all but the coldest UK gardens.

'Jean Marie de Montague' ►

'DONCASTER' Another of the popular Dutch reds. Dark-red flowers with a flare of black spots produced about 2 weeks later than those of 'Jean Marie'. There is often some bluish casting as the flower fades. Distinctive wavy-edged leaves. Compact and spreading with a relatively dwarf habit. Free-flowering from a young age and fairly easy to root. Readily available.

'KLUIS SENSATION' Frilled dark scarlet-red flowers in early June, on a compact slow-growing bush, smaller than 'JEAN MARIE', with pale-green leaves. Free-flowering, easily grown and widely available.

'KEN JANECK'
(*yakushimanum* hybrid)

H5 low May–early June 5

An excellent YAKUSHIMANUM hybrid which is unfortunately hard to root, and will only become widely distributed through tissue culture. Essentially this is like a pink-flowered version of the parent species, with more showy, flatter-faced flowers of pale pink which eventually fade out to white. More upright-growing than YAKUSHIMANUM and with similar, convex, thickly-indumented leaves. Good in full sun and hardy enough for any UK garden. So far, rather hard to obtain but bound to become popular.

'Kluis Sensation'

'Ken Janeck' A.E.

'YAKU PRINCESS' and the other 'Yaku' royal family including 'Yaku Prince' and 'Yaku Queen' are a group of eastern American hybrids hardy enough for any UK garden. They have foliage and habit very similar to that of their parent YAKUSHIMANUM, with convex indumented leaves. Ball-shaped trusses of apple-blossom pink, fading to white. Quite good, but sometimes rather shy-flowering as young plants, so they may be of limited popularity.

'KILIMANJARO'
(*elliottii* X 'Dusky Maid')

H4 medium late May–early June 6b

Named after the African mountain, this has some of the most spectacular flowers of all hybrids. Large currant-red flowers, spotted deep-crimson all over, in a huge wide truss of about 18. The red shade is one of the richest available, and the flowers do not fade. Unfortunately the plant has several drawbacks; it is hard to root, straggly and not always easy to please, although it is surprisingly hardy considering its parentage, surviving recent severe winters well in southern England. Rather hard to obtain and likely to remain a connoisseur's plant. F.C.C. 1947.

'RUBICON', named after the Roman river, is a hybrid of the above raised in New Zealand. The excellent pure-red flowers are similar to the above. Fine deep-green ribbed leaves on a plant of better habit than 'KILIMANJARO'. Less hardy than the above, and needs a sheltered site in light woodland. Becoming distributed through tissue-culture, and likely to become a popular enthusiast's plant.

'LADY CHAMBERLAIN' g.
(*cinnabarinum* Roylei X 'Royal Flush' Orange)

H3–(4) medium-tall early May 7a–(6b)

One of many hybrids raised from the species CINNABARINUM which passes on its clusters of pendulous, waxy, tubular flowers to its offspring. Small leaves on a slender, willowy, upright bush which can look rather bare, especially in exposed sites. There are several different-coloured clones available, the most common being: **'F.C.C.'** 1931—orange-salmon; **'Chelsea'**—orange-pink; **'Gleam'**—orange-yellow tipped crimson; **'Salmon Trout'**—salmon-pink. All are good, and although taking some years to flower freely, they put on a striking show as mature plants. These are woodland hybrids in climates similar to Glendoick, but can be grown in more open sites in the south and west. Not for the coldest gardens. The main problem with 'Lady Chamberlain', and her relations which follow, is their susceptibility to powdery mildew, which can defoliate or even kill plants if not controlled.

'BODNANT YELLOW' is a yellow version of 'Lady Chamberlain' with butter-yellow flowers, flushed orange and crimson. F.C.C. 1944.

'LADY ROSEBERY' *g.* is a pinker version of 'Lady Chamberlain' but is otherwise very similar. The F.C.C. 1932 clone with neyron rose flowers, deeper outside, is probably the only one now commercially available.

'TREWITHEN ORANGE' *g.* has waxy soft orange flowers. There are several different clones, the F.C.C. one being the most tender and slowest-growing.

'CINNKEYS' has very unusual clusters of orange and red tubular flowers, quite unlike any other hybrid. A.M. 1935.

'CONROY' has light-orange flowers, tipped rose. Fine glaucous leaves. A.M. 1950.

'LADY CLEMENTINE MITFORD'
(*maximum* hybrid)

H4–5 medium-tall June 6b–5/6a

Very old but still popular. Flowers peach-pink at the edges paling to blush white in the centre, spotted reddish-brown, in a compact rounded truss. Dark foliage, silvery when young, on a vigorous, spreading but dense plant, broader than tall. A faithful bloomer, tolerant of heat and sun. One of the best of the old Waterer hybrids. A.M.T. 1971. Readily available.

'LADY ELEANOR CATHCART' Even older than the above, but still quite popular. Clear pale-pink flowers with a narrow dark maroon flare in a rather small rounded truss. Distinctive long down-pointing leaves. Hardy in any UK garden. Quite readily available.

'LAMPION'
('Bad Eilsen' X *yakushimanum*)

H5 semi-dwarf mid-May 5

The name means a Chinese lantern. A very dense grower, one of the most compact 'yak' hybrids. Light-red bell-shaped flowers with paler centres on long flower stalks which fade to a paler shade, giving a two-tone effect. Dark shiny leaves. A promising, hardy, newly distributed German hybrid, distinct from most other 'yak' hybrids that we have seen.

'CUPCAKE' (*yakushimanum* x 'Medusa') has claret-rose buds which open to nearly full trusses of 10–15 carmine-rose/salmon-pink flowers, fading to paler inside. Very compact and dwarf, free-flowering and flowering earlier than the main group of 'yak' hybrids. Recently introduced from USA.

'LAVENDER GIRL'
(*fortunei* X 'Lady Grey Egerton')

H5 medium-tall late May 5/6a

Probably the most popular of the larger-growing, lavender-flowered hybrids. Full, dome-shaped trusses of scented, pale-lavender flowers, lighter in the centre. Glossy leaves on a vigorous, tough, easily grown plant, good in exposed sites. Hardy anywhere in the UK, and a fine plant, one of the best of this shade. F.C.C. 1967.

'MRS CHARLES PEARSON' is an even tougher hybrid of a similar colour, but without scent. Tall conical trusses of pinkish mauve flowers, opening in the first half of May. Hardy, vigorous and upright, forming a tidy bush, but we find it shy-flowering as a young plant. Not everyone's colour, but an easy plant for anywhere in Britain. F.C.C.T. 1955.

'SUSAN' is a fine hybrid with cool bluish-mauve flowers in early May. Fine deep-green leaves, rounded at the ends on a plant of tidy habit. Unfortunately hard to root, and usually grafted. Quite widely available. F.C.C.T. 1954.

'LAVENDULA'
([*russatum* X *saluenense*] X *rubiginosum*)

H5 low early May 5

An excellent German hybrid which resembles a dwarf version of its parent RUBIGINOSUM. Deep-lavender flowers with darker spots. Small aromatic, scaly leaves, on a vigorous but compact plant which is very easy to grow, hardy enough for anywhere in the UK and is ideal for the back of a dwarfs border.

'LEM'S CAMEO'
('Dido' X 'Anna')

H3–4 medium early May 7a–6b

Described in the USA as 'The Cadillac of the Industry' this is one of the finest connoisseur's hybrids ever raised. Large

'Lem's Cameo' S.P.A.

ball-shaped trusses of 17–20 frilled flowers fade through a mixture of pink, apricot and cream, blotched and spotted red in the throat. Thick foliage, bronzy when young, on a fairly compact but sometimes rather sparse bush. It is hard to propagate, and does not branch well, leading to a shortage of cutting and grafting material. It is also one of the greediest hybrids for fertilizer, its leaves turning yellow, unless it is fed several times a year. Likely to remain an enthusiast's plant, but one of the most striking of all hybrids, and well worth searching for. Not for the coldest gardens. S.P.A. 1971.

'NANCY EVANS' not surprisingly 'LEM'S CAMEO has been used as a parent, and this is one of the first of its many offspring to become available in the UK. Huge, packed trusses of hose-in-hose deep-yellow flowers, shaded orange on the outside and in the centre. Brownish young growth on a plant of good habit. Best in light woodland with some shelter, and not for the coldest gardens.

'Gartendirektor Glocker'

'LEM'S MONARCH'
('Anna' X 'Marinus Koster')

H4 tall mid-May 6b

This giant hybrid is one of a group known in the USA as the 'Wallopers'. These all have enormous trusses of shades of pink and white, and form massive domed shrubs which need plenty of room. 'Lem's Monarch' is probably the best of all, with tall conical trusses of white flowers, each rimmed with pink, giving a picotee effect. Very thick foliage on a sturdy plant which is free-flowering from about 5 years old, and is very reliable for us. Takes a fair amount of exposure, and suitable for all but the coldest UK gardens. If you have plenty of room, this is one of the most spectacular hybrids available.

◄ 'Lem's Monarch'

'EL CAMINO' Rosy-red flowers, darker in the throat, in a large truss. Habit and appearance as above. Needs some wind shelter for best results. The best of the deeper-coloured 'Wallopers', but somewhat prone to powdery mildew.

'LINDA'
(*williamsianum* X 'Britannia')

H5 low early May 5

Hybrids of the species WILLIAMSIANUM are easily recognized by their dense habit, rounded leaves and bell-shaped, pink flowers. This species has been much used as a parent, especially in continental Europe; 'Linda', raised in Holland, is one of the most popular. Nearly rounded trusses of frilled-rose pink flowers. Egg-shaped pale-green leaves on a dense bush forming

a compact mound. Best in full sun for best habit, and hardy enough for anywhere in the UK, although occasionally vulnerable to spring frosts. Widely available, reliable and easy.

'GARTENDIREKTOR GLOCKER' rather a mouthful for English speakers, is a fine WILLIAMSIANUM hybrid from West Germany. Rosy-red bell-shaped flowers in a small truss. Curious downwards-curving leaves. Very hardy, suitable for any UK garden. Becoming quite widely available.

'LIONEL'S TRIUMPH'
(*lacteum* X 'Naomi')

H4/5 medium-tall early May 6b–6a

Many hybridizers have used the superb species *LACTEUM* to produce hybrids with large trusses of yellow flowers. Pink buds open to 18 flower trusses of clear creamy yellow, flushed pink, and spotted crimson in the throat. Unfortunately *lacteum* passes on its well-known miffiness to its offspring. Hard to root and tends to have yellow foliage in gardens which do not have very acid soil. Usually a leggy grower and not always very free-flowering. Despite these problems, it is a worthy collector's plant with fine flowers, and a surprisingly tough constitution, thriving in some of the severer Scottish gardens. Not a plant for the beginner, and usually hard to obtain commercially. Other *lacteum* hybrids occasionally available and which have fine flowers but similar shortcomings include:

'BEATRICE KEIR'; yellow flowers with a greenish tinge. A.M. 1974.

'FRED ROSE'; clear lemon-yellow flowers, spotted red. H.C. 1973.

◄ 'Lionel's Triumph' F.C.C.

'Loderi King George' F.C.C.

'LODERI' g.
(*griffithianum* X *fortunei*)

H3/4 tall May 7a–6b

This is one of the most famous hybrids ever raised; more than 30 different selections have been made from it, although only a few of them are now commonly commercially available in the UK. White to pale-pink sweetly-scented flowers in loose trusses of 9–12. Large thin, smooth leaves, on purple stalks, tending sometimes to spotting and chlorosis. A tall, tree-forming hybrid which is not free-flowering until 5–8 years of age, but reliable thereafter. The most popular of all the scented hybrids, and now quite widely available through tissue-culture. Not for the coldest gardens, and needs light shade and shelter from wind to do well. The many clones available are all fairly similar and most are good. The most common ones are: 'GAME CHICK'. Pale pink with a faint blotch, slightly later than the others. 'KING GEORGE'. The most popular of the white clones. F.C.C. 1970. 'VENUS'. Light-pink flowers. The most popular of the pink clones.

'Loder's White' A.M.

'ALBATROSS' g. A hybrid of the above, useful for its later (June) flowering. Similar flowers to 'LODERI', with deeper throat markings, and similar in habit and appearance. Several clones exist, the most commonly available being **'A.M.'** with blush-pink flowers. Quite widely available. A.M.T. 1953.

'LODER'S WHITE'
(*griffithianum* hybrid)

H4 medium-tall early May 6b

Large conical trusses of pure white, edged pink and spotted red. Good in sun or light shade, very free-flowering, easy and reliable. Hardy in all but the coldest gardens, although it suffered some damage in Kent in recent severe winters and it sometimes drops its leaves in coldest weather. One of the most popular large white hybrids, and widely available. A.M. 1911.

'BEAUTY OF LITTLEWORTH', a similar hybrid, one of the largest growing of all and its huge white trusses with red spotting are so large that they weigh down the foliage forming a spectacular but untidy sight. Healthy shiny leaves on a vigorous bush which needs plenty of room and is best as a background plant. Widely available, popular, and slightly hardier than 'Loder's White'. F.C.C. 1904, F.C.C.T. 1953.

'MARCHIONESS OF LANSDOWNE'
(*maximum* hybrid)

H5 low-medium June 5

Striking violet-rose flowers with a large maroon-black flare, in a compact dome-shaped truss of about 14. Useful for its long-lasting late flowers, and its toughness, being hardy enough for full exposure and in any UK garden. Rather a sparse sprawling plant, which benefits from some pruning for best results.

'MRS T.H. LOWINSKY' is another blotched hybrid, flowering at the same time, and of similar habit. Mauve buds open to flowers of orchid pink, fading to white, with a bold orange blotch. Hardy, free-flowering, easy and widely available.

'MARKEETA'S PRIZE'
('Loderi Venus' X 'Anna')

H4 medium-tall early May 6b

One of the best of the recently introduced American red hybrids. Large, heavily textured bright scarlet flowers in full trusses. Thick dark foliage on a very sturdy plant which grows larger and more upright than most of the Dutch reds such as 'JEAN MARIE DE MONTAGUE' and 'KLUIS SENSATION'. Easy to please and becoming quite widely available. Not for the coldest gardens, but has been hardy so far at Glendoick.

'Markeeta's Prize' ►

'Martha Isaacson' P.A.

'HALFDAN LEM'. A similar hybrid, also raised in western USA and named after its raiser who emigrated from Scandinavia. Huge red flowers (possibly the largest available in this colour) sometimes fading to cherry red, on a very vigorous bush which can get rather untidy. Free-flowering and easy, but perhaps not as good as 'Markeeta's Prize'.

'MARTHA ISAACSON'
(*occidentale* X 'Mrs Donald Graham')

H4–5 medium-tall June 6b–6a

This is an Azaleodendron, a cross between a hardy hybrid rhododendron and a deciduous azalea. Unusual, scented, white flowers with pink stripes in tight flat trusses. Reddish bronzy foliage which hangs and turns brown in a severe winter, often giving a bush an appearance of being dead. An upright grower, good as a background plant, which is easy to please, and is the best Azaleodendron we have seen. P.A. 1956.

'GLORY OF LITTLEWORTH'. The most popular of the British Azaleodendrons. Very striking creamy-white flowers with a bold orange blotch. Blue-grey semi-deciduous leaves on a plant which is usually sparse and lacking in vigour. Large healthy plants of this are rarely seen and it needs much encouragement to thrive, although we find it quite long-lived. A.M. 1911.

'MAY DAY' g.
(haematodes X *griersonianum)*

H3 low-medium May 7a

As this cross has been made in at least four gardens, it is very variable. Brilliant orange-scarlet to signal-red flowers with coloured calyces in lax trusses of about 8. Medium-to-dark green foliage with a thick, light-brown indumentum, on a generally compact, flat-topped to rounded bush. Roots easily, free-flowering, easily grown but not suitable for gardens colder than Glendoick where it sometimes suffers bark-split and frosted second growth. Widely available. A.M. 1932. The following are similar red hybrids.

'THOR' is an American hybrid which is considered by some to be an improvement on 'May Day'. Bright scarlet flowers. P.A. 1961.

'MATADOR' g. has darker flowers and less indumentum, and is less compact. The clones that we have tried are rather tender. F.C.C. 1946.

'TALLY HO' H2 A very fine late orange-scarlet, too tender for us at Glendoick, but very good in a sheltered southern or western garden. F.C.C. 1933.

'ROMANY CHAI' H4 is a fairly late deep red with a straggly habit. A.M. 1932.

'ROMANY CHAL' H3 is even later with glowing deep-red flowers. Upright and vigorous. F.C.C. 1937.

'MERGANSER'
(campylogynum white x *luteiflorum)*

H4 semi-dwarf May 6b

Named after a species of duck, this rather unusual hybrid of our own raising has three flower trusses of pale primrose-yellow, like a yellow CAMPYLOGYNUM. Compact with dark-green leaves. Easy to root, buds up young and easy to grow. Very attractive, unusual and becoming quite widely available. H.C.T. 1981.

'TEAL', named after another duck, is larger in all parts with pale clear-primrose-yellow flowers. Upright to about 3ft (1m). A.M. 1977.

'Merganser' H.C.T.

'Fantastica'

'MOLLY ANN'
('Elizabeth' X garden hybrid)

H5 semi-dwarf May 5

Not for purists perhaps, but this is one of the best dwarfs we have seen for foliage and habit. Heavily textured, long-lasting flowers in a lax truss of about 7. Dark, shiny, rounded leaves on an upright but compact, very dense and tidy plant. Buds very young and roots easily. Unfortunately rather susceptible to powdery mildew. Becoming quite widely available.

'MOONSHINE' g.
('Adriaan Koster' X *wardii* Litiense)

H4 medium-tall early May 6b

A grex of popular yellow hybrids which we feel will soon be superseded by some of the new American and European introductions. Deep green glossy foliage on upright bushes which can become sparse and untidy. Not for gardens colder than Glendoick without a sheltered, favourable site. The named clones are: **A.M.** 1952—primrose-yellow flowers, with a crimson blotch; **'Bright'**—pale lemon-yellow flowers, tidy habit, needs good drainage; **'Crescent'**—primrose-yellow flowers on rather open plant, the best clone in our opinion, A.M.T. 1960; **'Supreme'**—primrose-yellow, dark glossy foliage. We find the buds tend to abort, but this may be a local problem. A.M.T. 1953.

'ELSIE STRAVER' A Dutch hybrid from a similar parentage, which is tougher than the 'Moonshine' g. but which tends to have rather poor yellowy foliage. Creamy-yellow flowers, with a deep-red blotch. Rather a leggy grower, which needs full sun. Not for the very coldest gardens.

'DAIRYMAID' has creamy yellow flowers tinged pink. Needs full sun to flower. Compact, and quite tough, but flowers are pale. A.M.T. 1934.

'LOGAN DAMARIS' has clear lemon-yellow flowers. Foliage has some tendency to yellowing. Quite good, and fairly widely available. A.M. 1948.

'MOONSTONE' g.
(*campylocarpum* X *williamsianum*)

H4 semi-dwarf-low May 6b

There are several different clones of this hybrid around. Rosy-crimson to yellow buds open to creamy-yellow bell-shaped flowers in a loose truss of 3–5. Some clones are cream or/and pink. Oval leaves on a fairly compact plant which roots quite easily. Blooms at 3–5 years with dainty but not spectacular flowers. Early growth is frost prone. Widely available.

'COWSLIP' is similar with pale-yellow to cream flowers with pink to red markings. A.M. 1937.

'GARTENDIREKTOR RIEGER' is a promising new German introduction with large cream-tinged rose flowers and rather handsome rounded foliage. Becoming available.

'Sneezy' A.M.T.

'MORGENROT' ('MORNING RED')
(*yakushimanum* x '*Spitfire*')

H5 low May–June 5

Dark red buds open to rose-red flowers, flushed deeper on the outside, which fade to pale rose, in a full truss of 16–18. Good dark foliage, with very thin indumentum on a compact, rounded plant. Hardy, suitable for any UK garden, and best in full sun. Quite easily rooted, buds at 2–3 years and should become popular.

'FANTASTICA' Striking two-toned flowers, opening red, shading inwards to a white throat. We feel that this is one of the best 'yak' hybrids we have seen. Newly introduced.

'SNEEZY' has compact trusses of rose-red flowers from a young age. A vigorous, upright grower with dull-green foliage with no indumentum. Very hardy. A.M.T. 1986.

'Naomi Exbury' A.M.

'SURREY HEATH' Rose-pink flowers with a creamy centre, giving a two-toned effect. Leaves have white tomentum above on the new growth. Tends to have yellow leaves. Free-flowering and widely available. A.M.T. 1982.

'MRS A.T. DE LA MARE'
(*fortunei* 'Sir Charles Butler' X 'Halopeanum')

H5 medium-tall May–June 5

A fine, rightly popular, hardy hybrid with slightly fragrant, frilled, 12–14-flower, lax trusses opening from pale pink to pure white, with a ray of green spots in the throat. Smaller flowers and trusses than 'LODERI' but much hardier and tolerant of less sheltered conditions. Flowers are somewhat thin-textured and mark easily in sun or rain. Glossy foliage on a tidy but upright growing plant. Readily available. A.M. 1958.

◄ 'Surrey Heath' A.M.T.

'NAOMI' g.
('Aurora' x *fortunei*)

H4–5 medium-tall May 6b–6a

One of the best known of the Exbury hybrids. The various clones have fragrant flowers with lax trusses of shades of pink, yellow and white. A tall grower, forming a small tree which is an impressive sight in full flower. Shiny rounded leaves. Most clones are not free-flowering as young plants and are hard to root. Hardy, but best with some wind shelter, and somewhat prone to powdery mildew. The following clones are the best and are fairly widely available: **'Exbury'** A.M. 1933—pale lilac-pink shading to yellow and white in the centre; **'Nautilus'** A.M. 1938—frilled flowers, rose flushed pale orange, paling in the centre; **'Stella maris'** F.C.C. 1939—lilac-pink in rather poor trusses.

'Nova Zembla'

'NOBLEANUM' g.
(*caucasicum* X *arboreum*)

H4 medium December–March 6b

This is the best known early-flowering hybrid, and there are many clones in commerce; some of much better colour with better trusses than others. Most have flowers of scarlet-pink to scarlet-rose, usually with a hint of blue, spotted red to crimson, in full to rather loose trusses of 10–20. The leaves have some smooth indumentum below. It can open its first flowers before Christmas but in colder climates, usually not until February–March. All flower relatively young and root easily. Apart from the various forms of 'Nobleanum' itself, the following are usually available. **'Nobleanum album'**—white to blush flowers spotted greenish-yellow; **'Nobleanum coccineum'**—bright crimson-rose flowers; **'Nobleanum venustum'**—pink flowers with a white centre, spotted. None have spectacular flowers but all are worth growing for their earliness.

◄ 'Nobleanum'

'NOVA ZEMBLA'
('Parson's Grandiflorum' X hardy red hybrid)

H5 medium May–June 5

This is perhaps the most widely grown and successful red hybrid for severe climates and so is ideal for the coldest parts of the UK. Dark red flowers, slightly blue-tinged, darker spots in a full rounded truss. Deep-green healthy leaves on a sturdy upright grower.

'Odee Wright'

'ODEE WRIGHT'
('Idealist' x 'Mrs Betty Robertson')

H4 low-medium May 6b

Better than either parent, this is a fine yellow raised in north-west USA which has done well at Glendoick. Peach buds open to flowers of chartreuse/primrose yellow, tinged pink, spotted carmine in the throat, in trusses of 12–15. Glossy, deep-green leaves on a compact and dense plant. Fairly easy to root, buds up young and good for climates similar to and milder than our own. Becoming more widely available. A.M. 1990.

'DINY DEE' is a new hybrid with deeper-yellow flowers. Mildew-prone.

'PATTY BEE'
(*keiskei* 'Yaku Fairy' x *fletcherianum*)

H5 dwarf April 5/6a

An excellent, easily grown dwarf yellow. Clear, pale-yellow, unspotted flowers in a truss of about 6. A compact mounded plant. Very free-flowering and easy to root. Flowers not quite as large or as deep-coloured as 'CURLEW', but the plant is hardier and easier to please and should be growable in all UK gardens, although early flowers are susceptible to frost. Becoming widely available. S.P.A. 1985. A.M.T. 1989.

'PRINCESS ANNE' is another hardy, easily grown dwarf with small pale-yellow flowers in May. Foliage bronzy when young, and sometimes bronzy in the winter.

'Patty Bee' S.P.A./A.M.T.

Widely available, and easy to grow, best in full sun. F.C.C.T. 1983.

'PENJERRICK' g.
(campylocarpum X griffithianum)

H3 tall April–May 7a

Named after the Cornish garden where it was raised, this has been considered by some to be the most gracefully beautiful of all hybrids but it needs a fairly mild sheltered woodland site. It survives with us but can suffer badly in severe winters. There are several colour forms, including cream, creamy yellow, pale yellow flushed pink, and pale pink; all have bell-shaped flowers in a very lax truss of about 7. Fairly glossy medium-green leaves on an upright open tree-like plant. Rather hard to root. Some clones are usually available. A.M. 1923.

'CORNISH CROSS' g. is another large-growing woodland hybrid of similar hardiness. Deeper-coloured flowers, from deep pink to red, fading to shades of pink, giving a bi-colour effect. Fine bark. Very susceptible to powdery mildew.

'Percy Wiseman' A.M.T.

'PERCY WISEMAN'
([*yakushimanum* x 'Fabia Tangerine'] selfed)??

H4–5 low May–early June 6b–6a

Named after its raiser, this is one of the most popular 'yak' hybrids. Showy, multi-coloured flowers, peach-pink and cream, fading to creamy white with a yellow throat and green marks, in a rounded truss. A fairly compact, vigorous, well-branched plant which buds up young and roots easily. A distinctive plant, becoming very popular and now widely available. A.M.T. 1981.

'BAMBI' has soft-pink flowers, tinged with yellow, fading out quickly. Good foliage with some indumentum. Not the most compact 'yak' hybrid.

'PINK DRIFT'
(*calostrotum* X *polycladum*)

H5 dwarf April–May 5

A hardy dwarf hybrid with magenta-pink funnel-shaped flowers in trusses of about 3. A very dense and compact grower, best in full sun. One of the hardiest and freest flowering dwarfs. Not everyone's colour, but easy to please and recommended for the beginner. Widely available.

'PINK PEARL'
('George Hardy' x 'Broughtonii')

H4 tall May–June 6b

Probably the most famous hybrid of all. Conical trusses of about 18 flowers open soft pink and fade to near white, with brown speckling. Thick, pale but healthy foliage on an upright plant, straggly if not in full sun. Too large and too fast-growing for many small modern gardens, where less vigorous pinks such as some of the 'yak' hybrids are preferable. Easily rooted and buds up young. Still very widely available. F.C.C. 1900.

'ALICE' is a hybrid of the above with deep pink flowers, lighter in the centre, which fade to near white. Does not bud up as well as 'Pink Pearl', but equally fine in flower, and widely available. A.M. 1910.

'BETTY WORMALD' similar but slightly less vigorous than 'Pink Pearl' and holds its pink colour better. F.C.C.T. 1964.

'MOTHER OF PEARL' is a sport of 'Pink Pearl' differing only in its flower colour, opening pale pink, fading quickly to white flushed lavender-pink. A.M. 1930.

'TRUDE WEBSTER' a similar American hybrid with large conical trusses of thick-textured deep-pink flowers which fade to near white. Robust with thick foliage, forming a fairly tidy plant in full sun. Becoming quite widely available. S.P.A. 1971.

'Betty Wormald' F.C.C.T.

'Trude Webster' S.P.A.

'P.J. MEZITT/'P.J.M.'
(*minus* Carolinianum X *dauricum*)

H5 low March–April 5

This extremely hardy, small-leaved hybrid is extremely popular in climates severer than that of the UK, and is well worth planting here for early colour. Medium rosy-purple, long-lasting, somewhat frost-hardy flowers in trusses of 4–9. Small leaves turn mahogany in winter on a upright compact bush. Best in a sunny site to flower freely. One of the hardiest rhododendrons ever raised, tolerating −25°F/−32°C, so never likely to be damaged anywhere in the UK. Wind- and drought-resistant, so can be planted in inhospitable sites. Several clones exist, but the variation is slight, and most are worth growing. A.M. 1972.

'POLAR BEAR' g.
(*diaprepes* X *auriculatum*)

H4 tall July–August 6b

Many late-flowering white hybrids have been raised using the species AURICULATUM, and 'Polar Bear' is one of the most popular. Flat-topped trusses of strongly fragrant, trumpet-shaped, white flowers, sometimes marked green or brown. Thin, long, smooth leaves on a very large, tree-like shrub which needs shelter from wind, and its flowers last better in light shade. Many clones were distributed, some better than others, and there is considerable variation in flowering times. Most are reasonably good, but avoid those with chlorotic foliage. We find this easy to grow and we would recommend 'Polar Bear' or its related hybrids in northern and eastern gardens, rather than AURICULATUM itself which tends to grow late and suffer damage from early frosts.

'LODAURIC' is a similar hybrid which flowers a couple of weeks earlier than 'Polar Bear' and has more sun-resistant flowers. The most commonly sold clone in the UK is **'Iceberg'** A.M. 1958.

◄ 'PJM Elite'

'PRAECOX'
(*ciliatum* X *dauricum*)

H4–5 low-medium March 6b–6a

'Praecox' is Latin for 'early' and this is one of the most popular early flowering hybrids. Trusses with 2–3 flowers of rosy-purple. Small thin scaly leaves on an upright plant which responds well to pruning and which can be used as an informal hedge. In the very severest climates, 'P. J. MEZITT' which is hardier and later-flowering may be a better bet. F.C.C. 1978.

'EMASCULUM', from the same cross, has a more upright habit than 'Praecox', is later flowering, and is lighter-coloured. We find that it tends to have a poor root system and have given up propagating it. Said to have a degree of alkalinity tolerance. A.M. 1976.

'TESSA' g. is not as hardy as its parent 'Praecox', but has larger, more impressive flowers. **'Tessa'** A.M. 1935 has purplish-pink flowers, **'Tessa Roza'** has finer deep-rose-pink flowers. A.M. 1953.

'BO-PEEP', for milder areas, provides an excellent contrast to the above hybrids and their parent species. Pale greenish-yellow flowers in clusters, on an erect plant which can be rather sparse. Easy to root, free-flowering and widely available. Barely hardy in eastern Scotland, suffering bark-split, but very successful in southern and western parts of Britain. Susceptible to mildew. A.M. 1934.

'PRESIDENT ROOSEVELT'
(parentage unknown)

H4 medium early May 6b

This is the most spectacular of the few variegated rhododendrons which exist. Smooth green leaves have bold flashes of

'Ptarmigan' F.C.C.

yellow variegation, and the striking flowers are bright red fading to white in the centre, in conical trusses. Unfortunately we find the plant floppy and brittle, weak on its roots and very inclined to revert, requiring the green shoots to be cut out to avoid losing the variegation completely. It may do better as a grafted plant. Sometimes suffers frost damage here, and not for the coldest gardens. Despite its drawbacks, this is sufficiently unusual to make it worth growing if you like its unusual leaves.

'GOLDFLIMMER', a newly introduced German hybrid, has similar yellow variegation to 'President Roosevelt', on a much sturdier, more compact, easily grown, very hardy hybrid. The flowers are a rather average PONTICUM mauve pink in small tight trusses. Likely to become widely grown. See also *PONTICUM* 'VARIEGATUM'.

'PTARMIGAN'
(*orthocladum* var. *microleucum* X *leucaspis*)

H4 dwarf-semi dwarf March 6b

Named after the Snow Grouse, this is one of the most popular of our own hybrids. Pure white flowers in clusters on a spreading plant with small dark leaves, which eventually forms a compact mound. The flowers will stand a little frost, and open over a period of several weeks in mild early spring weather. Very free-flowering and easy to grow, but not for severest areas with regular spring frosts. F.C.C. 1965.

'PURPLE SPLENDOUR'
(*ponticum* hybrid)

H4–5 low-medium late May–early June 6b–5/6a

This is probably the most striking purple hybrid ever raised. Very frilled satiny, deep-purplish-blue flowers with an almost black blotch in the centre, in trusses of about 15. Deep-green shiny leaves on an upright bush somewhat lacking in vigour; often over-flowering, it needs a good site to thrive. Somewhat susceptible to mildew. Probably hardy enough for any UK garden; and the flowers are such a magnificent shade that it's a must for any hybrid collection. A.M. 1931.

'Purple Splendour' A.M. ►

'Razorbill' F.C.C.T.

'RAMAPO'
(*fastigiatum* X *minus* Carolinianum)

H5 semi-dwarf April–May 5

This is probably the hardiest of all the dwarf 'blues', and will easily take the worst winters of the severest areas of the UK. Pale pinkish violet-blue flowers in small trusses. Forms a compact impenetrable mound if planted in full sun, and has excellent dusty grey-blue foliage. Free-flowering, easy to please and an excellent landscape dwarf, planted in clumps. The flowers are not as good as the less hardy dwarfs such as 'INTRIFAST', 'SONGBIRD' etc. but the foliage is excellent, and the plant is far tougher.

'MOERHEIM' is a very hardy Dutch dwarf 'blue' with clusters of pale violet-blue flowers. Glossy dark-green pointed leaves, which turn bronzy in winter, on a compact spreading plant. Flowers pale and rather unspectacular, but this is another very easily grown hybrid which should withstand winters anywhere in the UK.

'RAZORBILL'
(*spinuliferum* X)

H4 semi-dwarf April 6b

Named after a seabird, this is becoming one of the most popular of our own hybrids due to its very unusual flowers. Up-pointing clusters of tubular, long-lasting, rose-pink flowers on a compact spreading bush with unusual crinkly leaves. To date, this is the hardiest and most compact of the hybrids raised from the unusual species *spinuliferum*. Sometimes hard to root, and not always as easily obtainable as it should be. Recommended for all but the coldest gardens. F.C.C.T. 1983.

'SETA' H3 (7a) is another well-known and popular *spinuliferum* hybrid with striking widely tubular light-pink flowers, with deeper stripes down the outside. Unfortunately we find its March-opening flowers are very easily frosted and the plant

'Riplet' A.M.T.

itself often suffers severe bark-split. As a young plant it tends to be sparse and straggly, but it fills in as it gets older. Susceptible to powdery mildew. Very successful in southern and western gardens, and worth risking in gardens further north and east, but not in areas colder than Glendoick. F.C.C. 1960.

'RIPLET'
(*forrestii* Repens X 'Letty Edwards')

H4 low April 6b

One of our favourite smaller USA hybrids, this has open-topped trusses of relatively large red flowers which fade to pale translucent pink, giving a two-tone effect. Stiff branches hold small leaves on a fairly compact plant. Best in light woodland, to protect its flowers from spring frosts. Needs good drainage, resents fertilizer and is somewhat prone to powdery mildew. Not for the coldest or more exposed gardens, but a worthy hybrid for the enthusiast. 'LAMPION' is a smaller-flowered but hardier hybrid of similar colouring. H.C.T. 1986.

'RUBY HART'
(['Carmen' X Elizabeth'] X *elliottii*)

H3–4 low early May 7a–6b

A fine medium-sized hybrid which we introduced from the USA. Not for gardens colder than Glendoick, but pretty reliable here, only suffering in the severest winters. Very dark red, long-lasting, waxy flowers in a lax truss. Fine deep-green ribbed foliage on a compact well-clothed plant. Buds young and free-flowering. A.M. 1988.

'Maricee' A.E./A.M.T.

'BUKETTA' is a German hybrid with ruby-red flowers, slightly paler than the above, on a hardier, compact, free-flowering plant which should be chosen in preference to 'Ruby Hart' for colder or less favourable gardens than Glendoick. We find it easy and reliable, and it will probably become widely grown.

'SAPPHO'
(unknown)

H5 tall May–June 5

Still the best known and most popular blotched white. Mauve buds open to white flowers, with a contrasting large purple-black flare, in a medium-sized, conical truss. Dark, rather narrow foliage on a vigorous, upright, leggy plant, which needs full sun for an acceptable habit. Roots easily and free-flowering from 3–4 years. There are new dwarfer hybrids of this type becoming available which may take its place. Widely available. A.M.T. 1974.

'SARLED'
(*sargentianum* X *trichostomum*)

H4 dwarf-semi dwarf May 6b

Light-pink buds open to creamy-white, long-lasting, daphne-like flowers in a small truss of about 7. Tiny narrow leaves on a dense compact plant. Easier to root and considerably easier to grow than its parents, making it a good beginners' plant. Readily available. A.M. 1974.

'MARICEE' has similar creamy-white flowers and contrasting dark foliage. Less dense and taller than the above. Recommended. A.M.T. 1983.

◄ 'Sappho' A.M.T.

'Elisabeth Hobbie' A.M.T

'SCARLET WONDER'
('Essex Scarlet' x *forrestii* Repens)

H5 semi dwarf-low May 5

This dwarf red has become one of the most popular of all hybrids. Bright cardinal-red, wavy-edged flowers in a loose truss of 4–7. Glossy, ribbed foliage, with some tendency to yellowing, on a compact but uneven plant which grows wider than high. Easily rooted and free-flowering from two years or less. Very hardy and suitable for any UK climate. One of the most widely available hybrids. H.C.T. 1970. The following are from the same cross.

'ELISABETH HOBBIE' is similar in flower but does not bud up as young. With us it makes a better plant, with deeper-green, healthier leaves. A.M.T. 1986.

'BADEN BADEN' is very free-flowering with slightly darker flowers. Wavy dark leaves on a compact plant which can become sparse with age. H.C.T. 1972. There are many other clones of this German cross available, all rather similar. The most popular of these are: **'Aksel Olsen'**, **'Bengal'**, and **'Spring Magic'**.

'SCINTILLATION'
(*fortunei* X)

H5 medium mid-May 5

An excellent very hardy hybrid from eastern USA which has recently become widely available in the UK. Pastel-pink flowers, with a brown and pink flare, in a rounded truss of about 15. Dark glossy foliage on a sturdy, well-shaped but not dense bush. One of the best American hybrids, free-flowering, hardy anywhere in the UK, but may suffer wind damage in very exposed sites. A.E. 1973. The following, also raised by Charles Dexter in Massachussets, are similar in foliage, habit and hardiness.

'Scintillation' A.E.

'BEN MOSELEY' is light purplish pink, with a crimson flare. Smaller, paler leaves than 'Scintillation'.

'BROWN EYES' has unusual flowers, rose-pink with a bold brown blotch.

'Ben Moseley'

'Seven Stars' F.C.C.

'SEVEN STARS'
('Loderi Sir Joseph Hooker' X *yakushimanum*)

H4–5 low-medium May 6b–5/6a

One of the finest YAKUSHIMANUM hybrids in flower, this has pale-pink to white flowers, flushed red-purple, in rounded trusses. The flowers have a light but definite scent, derived from the 'LODERI' parentage. One of the tallest of all YAKUSHIMANUM hybrids, the original plants are now over 12ft (3.6m) high, but it is fairly slow-growing. Shiny deep-green leaves on a compact dense plant, rather susceptible to powdery mildew. Hardy in all but the coldest gardens, where it will probably succeed in a favourable site. F.C.C. 1974. Other white YAKUSHIMANUM hybrids include:

'HACHMANN'S PORZELLAN', newly introduced from Germany, has white flowers with a yellow blotch, on a compact, hardy plant. Promising.

'SILVER SIXPENCE' has fine creamy-white flowers, with lemon spots, but poor foliage and habit, and it is rather slow to bud up. A.M.T. 1986.

'SIR CHARLES LEMON'
(*arboreum* X *campanulatum*)

H4–(5) medium-tall April 6b–(6a)

Pure white flowers, faintly spotted red, about 10 per conical truss. The foliage is amongst the finest of any hybrid. Stiff, matt, deep-green, ribbed leaves have cinnamon indumentum below, on a tidy but upright tree-like plant. Takes some years to flower, and hard to root, but now in tissue culture, so it should become more widely available. Proving to be hardier than previously thought, and should be planted in gardens where pure ARBOREUM is too tender. Probably hardy with some shelter in almost any UK garden, although the early flowers and growth are susceptible to frosts.

'SNIPE'

(*pemakoense* X *davidsonianum*)

H3 semi-dwarf April 7a

Another one of our 'bird' hybrids. Pale-pink flowers with lavender tinges and spotting. Very free-flowering, covering the foliage completely. Pale-green leaves on a plant with the appearance of a tall *PEMAKOENSE*. Expanding buds and flowers are frost-tender. Easy to grow but not for gardens colder than Glendoick. A.M. 1975.

'PHALAROPE' is a sister seedling of 'Snipe' with slightly more purple in the flower. A.M.T. 1983.

'ROSE ELF' is a similar American hybrid, smaller and flowering slightly earlier than the above, with pastel-pink flowers, very freely produced. Compact, and easy to grow. Not for gardens colder than Glendoick.

'SONATA'

('Purple Splendour' X *dichroanthum*)

H4–5 low-medium June 6b–6a

Unusual orange flowers with claret centres in small open-topped trusses. Small, matt, blue-green leaves, on a very dense, fairly slow-growing plant, which stays compact in full sun. A somewhat unreliable flowerer when young, but free-flowering, once mature. This is hardier than most hybrids of this colour, and is suitable for almost all UK gardens, although it may need protection in the coldest ones. H.C.T. 1959.

'SEPTEMBER SONG' is a promising American hybrid of similar colour to the above, with larger flowers. Vigorous but fairly compact. Becoming available.

'September Song'

'SONGBIRD'
(*russatum* X 'Blue Tit')

H4–5 semi-dwarf April 6b–6a

One of the most satisfactory dwarf 'blues' for us, with glossy deep-green foliage which does not spot in winter. Clusters of deep violet-blue flowers open earlier than those of 'SAPPHIRE', 'BLUE DIAMOND' etc. Easy to grow, best in full sun, and very free-flowering, often opening some flowers in the autumn with us. A.M. 1957.

'SACKO' is a similar German hybrid which we find to be one of the best of all the dwarf 'blues' we have seen. Purple-blue flowers in clusters on a compact dense plant with healthy foliage. Later-flowering than 'SONGBIRD'.

'SAPPHIRE' A.M. has pale purplish-blue flowers on a relatively open bush. It is still widely grown and popular, but we have given it up, preferring **'Night Sky'**, which has similar flowers but better foliage and habit.

'TEMPLE BELLE' g.
(*williamsianum* X *orbiculare*)

H4 low April–early May 6b

'Temple Belle's parents both have rounded leaves and bell-shaped pink flowers, and not surprisingly these traits are passed on to the hybrid. Loose trusses of 3–5 pale-pink, rose-pink or lavender-pink flowers on a fairly compact plant with disc-like smooth rounded leaves. Best in light woodland, but not in too much shade, to avoid straggliness. The early flowers and growth are rather vulnerable to frosts. There are many clones of this hybrid around; some are decidedly poor and should be avoided. In coldest gardens, other hardier *WILLIAMSIANUM* hybrids such as 'LINDA', and 'GARTENDIREKTOR GLOCKER' are probably a better bet.

'PINK PEBBLE' is another WILLIAMSIANUM hybrid, lower-growing and more compact than the above, with loose trusses of 4–5 rosy-pink flowers. Buds up freely, and late into growth, avoiding spring frosts. Not for coldest gardens. One of our favourite *williamsianum* hybrids. A.M. 1975.

'TITAN BEAUTY'
([*facetum* X 'Fabia Tangerine'] X [*yakushimanum* X 'Fabia Tangerine'])??

H4 low May–early June 6b

Waxy turkey-red flowers which hold their colour well, in a fairly full truss. An upright but dense compact plant with deep-green leaves and thin brown indumentum. One of the best red *YAKUSHIMANUM* hybrids, but not as hardy as most, and probably not suitable for the coldest UK gardens.

'SKOOKUM' is a hardier, taller-growing *YAKUSHIMANUM* hybrid, newly introduced from America. Bright red flowers. The hardiest of the red *yakushimanum* hybrids in commerce, and suitable for any UK garden.

'TOO BEE/NOT TOO BEE' ('Wee Bee')
(*campylogynum* 'Patricia' X *keiskei* 'Yaku Fairy')

H5 Dwarf late April–early May 5/6a

Two very promising dwarf hybrids from the raiser of 'GINNY GEE'. Unfortunately the name 'Not Too Bee' is not allowed under the rules of nomenclature, and it is unfortunately to be changed to 'Wee Bee', an awful name. Both have red buds opening to trusses of 3–5 pendulous rose-pink flowers, deeper on the outside, spotted claret-rose. The main difference is that 'Not Too Bee' is slightly earlier into flower. Both very low-growing and compact with healthy deep-green leaves. Free-flowering and easy, and should be grown in full sun. Flowers may be prone to late frosts, but should be hardy anywhere in the UK. Becoming available. A.M. 1988. Both A.E. 1989.

'Unique' F.C.C.

'TORTOISESHELL' g.
('Goldsworth Orange' X *griersonianum*)

H3 medium late May–early June 6b

This is a grex of free-flowering pastel-coloured hybrids for milder gardens. Quite large, upright but fairly tidy growers, which should not be planted in too much shade to avoid straggliness. On the tender side for us at Glendoick, needing a sheltered site but very good in milder southern and western gardens. The most popular clones are: **'Tortoiseshell Champagne'**, pale yellow, tinged pink, A.M.T. 1967; **'Tortoiseshell Orange'**, orange-red, leaves have purple leaf stalks; **'Tortoiseshell Wonder'**, salmon-pink with some orange hues, pale leaves on purple leaf-stalks, the most popular clone in the UK, A.M. 1947.

'UNIQUE'
(*campylocarpum* hybrid)

H4 low-medium late April–early May 6b

One of the most popular hybrids of all, especially useful for its very dense, compact habit. Pink buds open to pale ochre-yellow flowers which fade to ivory flushed pink and yellow, in rounded trusses of about 14. Quite slow-growing, forming an impenetrable neat bush with rounded leaves, although in shade it can get straggly. Not hardy enough without some shelter in the very severest UK gardens, but hardy and tough in full exposure at Glendoick. Sometimes a little slow to start flowering, and the flower colour is rather indistinct, but an excellent landscape plant and deservedly popular. F.C.C. 1935.

'BRUCE BRECHTBILL' from western USA is a sport of 'Unique', with identical foliage and habit but differing in its light but bright pink flowers with yellow tinges. The flowers are more effective than those of 'Unique' and we prefer it. Becoming quite widely available.

'Vanessa Pastel' F.C.C.

'VANESSA PASTEL'
('Soulbut' X *griersonianum*)

H3–4 low-medium late May 7a–6b

'Vanessa' was the first of many hybrids raised from the red species GRIERSONIANUM to be exhibited, and 'Vanessa Pastel' is the best clone from this grex. Lax trusses of strong cream flowers, flushed pink at the edges, stained red on the outside, and in the throat. Free-flowering and compact, with long pale-green leaves. Not for gardens colder than Glendoick, and its late growth is vulnerable to early frosts. One of our favourite hybrids, and recommended wherever it can be grown. F.C.C. 1971.

'VIRGINIA RICHARDS'
([*wardii* X 'F.C. Puddle'] X 'Mrs Betty Robertson')

H4–5 medium-tall early May 6b–6a

Introduced by ourselves from the USA, this has proved to be one of the finest of all hybrids, and it never fails to impress in flower. Flowers open rosy pink, fading to apricot cream with a red centre, in large rounded trusses. Deep green leaves on a vigorous but tidy, bushy plant which sailed through our severe winter of 1981/82 and flowered perfectly in the following spring. Free-flowering and easy to grow. Its one problem is its susceptibility to powdery mildew which may hinder its popularity, especially in the west. Planted in an open site, the mildew problem is lessened. A.M.T. 1985.

'TIDBIT' is another bi-coloured American hybrid which we introduced into the UK Red buds open to lax trusses of straw yellow flowers with red throats and calyces. A neat, compact, dense, fairly low grower with pointed glossy leaves. Not as hardy as 'Virginia Richards' and not recommended for gardens much colder than Glendoick. Best results in light shade, in a well-drained site. H.C. 1977.

'VISCY'

('Diane' x *viscidifolium*)

H5 medium May–June 5

Long-lasting, heavily-textured large whisky-coloured (orange and yellow) flowers, with bold dark red spotting, 4–8 per open truss. Attractive, large, dark shiny ribbed foliage on a rather open plant. Rather a curiosity with most unusual flowers which always attract comment. One of the hardiest orange hybrids, and one of the few suitable for severest UK climates. Fair rootability and reasonably free-flowering. Becoming available in the UK.

'VULCAN'

('Mars' x *griersonianum*)

H5 medium June 5/6a

The God of Fire is one of the hardiest GRIERSONIANUM hybrids. Domed trusses of fiery blood-red. Long leaves on a compact but not very dense bush. Easy to root and buds up young. Should be hardy enough for anywhere in the UK, and best in plenty of light for a compact habit. There may be more than one clone in commerce. Quite readily available. A.M.T. 1957.

'WHISPERINGROSE'

(*williamsianum* x 'Elizabeth')

H4 semi-dwarf April 6b

Relatively large open bells of rich carnation rose-cherry red in lax trusses. Fine deep-green, rounded, veined leaves, bronzy when young. A very good dense compact grower, easy to root, buds up from two years of age and looks good all the year round. A fine hybrid, but probably not for gardens colder than Glendoick.

'LORI EICHELSER' has similar but smaller flowers and smoother foliage, and is hardier. Earlier flowering

'WIGEON'

(*minus* Carolinianum X *calostrotum* 'Gigha')

H5 semi-dwarf May

One of the hardiest Glendoick dwarfs. Saucer-shaped, deep-pink flowers with lavender tones, spotted deeper. Dusty grey-green leaves. Free-flowering, reasonably easy to root and easy to grow. Becoming quite widely available. A.M.T. 1987.

'CUTIE' grows a little taller with quantities of lilac flowers with pink shading, from multiple buds. Prone to rust fungus. A.E. 1962.

'WILGEN'S RUBY'

('Britannia' x 'John Walter')

H5 medium June 5

The standard red hybrid in north-west Europe, this has full trusses of bright red flowers, with brown spotting. Slow-growing and compact, with upward-curving leaves. Easy to root and free-flowering from a young age. A good hybrid for general cultivation and widely available. F.C.C. 1951.

'Winsome' A.M.

'WILSONI' (syn. 'Laetevirens')
(*minus* Carolinianum x *ferrugineum*)

H5 semi dwarf-low June 5

Small rosy-pink tubular flowers in a dense truss. Long dark leaves on a compact rounded bush. Roots fairly easily. Useful for its late flowers, hardiness, and tolerance of wind and poor soil conditions. Rather slow to bud up. Susceptible to leaf gall, and sometimes unstable on its roots. Quite widely available.

'WINSOME'
('Humming Bird' x *griersonianum*)

H4 low-medium May 6b

A fine medium-sized hybrid, hardy enough for most of the UK. Pointed reddish buds open to lax trusses of cherry-pink flowers. Dark-pointed leaves are bronzy when young. Compact and dense in the sun, more open in shade. Easy to root and buds up very young. One of the best of its kind. Widely available. A.M. 1950.

◄ 'Wilsoni'

'YELLOW HAMMER'
(*sulfureum* x *flavidum*)

H4 medium April–May 6b

Tiny, tubular, clear-yellow flowers from multiple buds, produced up the stems. Small, narrow, medium-green leaves on a narrow, upright, vigorous plant, straggly with age. Roots easily and free-flowering from 3–4 years. Often blooms in autumn as well as spring. The often necessary pruning may be done in flower for house decoration. Widely available.

'FOLIAGE HYBRIDS'

(using species such as BUREAVII, PACHYSANTHUM, YAKUSHIMANUM, PROTEOIDES, LANATUM, FICTOLACTEUM and many others).

Crosses between two species invariably produce fairly uniform seedlings. We and others have found that hybrids between species with fine foliage (e.g. thick indumentum above and below the leaves, in various shades of white, fawn and brown) are very good value, even as unselected seedlings. They generally flower at a younger age than their parents, are easier to please, and are often capable of taking more exposure. Many of these hybrids combine the foliage or/and flower qualities of their parents to give plants of equal or superior ornamental value. In a few cases, the hybrids are a poor compromise between their parents, but as a general rule most of these crosses, made with the best forms of the species, are a bonus to a collection. Crosses between YAKUSHIMANUM and tender-large-leaved species often produce hardy dwarfer versions of the latter. These should flower at 4–8 years of age, rather than 10–30 years which is common for some large-leaved species such as SINOGRANDE and FALCONERI.

DECIDUOUS AZALEAS

Mass of deciduous azaleas

Unlike most rhododendrons, these plants lose their leaves in the winter, and so are not as useful in general landscaping as their evergreen relations, although many of them do have striking autumn colour. There are many species of deciduous azalea, found in Japan, China, Turkey, North America and elsewhere, and many of these have been used in breeding a vast array of popular hybrids. Both the species and the hybrids are well worth growing.

LUTEUM

H4–5 low-medium May–June 6b–5

Also known as the pontic or ponticum azalea, this is a very well-known plant which has naturalized itself in some southern and western parts of the UK, although it is nothing like as invasive as the rhododendron species PONTICUM which comes from a similar area of the Caucasus. *Luteum* is also found in Yugoslavia and Austria, and is the only European native azalea. The yellow, sweetly scented flowers appear before the leaves, and the flowers often open over a long period. The leaves turn scarlet in autumn before they fall. Very versatile and easy to please, growing in more shade than almost any rhododendron, and should be hardy enough for all but the very severest UK gardens. One of the parent species of many of the deciduous azalea hybrids, and has been used as an understock for grafting these although this is not common practice now. Widely available.

JAPONICUM

H4–5 low-medium May–June 6b–6a

(This species was formerly sometimes known as *molle*, which name is correctly applied to a different species from China.) A Japanese species, it has been much used in breeding. Clusters of large, usually salmon-pink flowers in May. Pink or yellow strains are occasionally available. Sometimes has fine autumn colours but usually has little or no scent.

OCCIDENTALE

H4 low-medium June–July 6b

An excellent western American species, which is especially useful for its late flowering. Sweetly scented white flowers, often tinged pink and blotched yellow. This description fits the typical species, but many unusual forms have been collected recently with interesting variations such as very frilled flowers and reddish, deep-pink or yellow-tinged or blotched flowers. We have been building a collection of these over the years, which now numbers over 50 different variations. We have propagated about 12 of them under their collectors' numbers, and now other nurseries are offering them. It is well worth making a collection of some of these if you have room. They seem to put up with damper conditions than most rhododendrons, but we find that they also do very well in a fairly dry site in full sun. Some clones hang onto their green foliage through much of the winter, while others turn yellow or scarlet in the autumn. Used in hybridizing, its offspring include the azaleodendron 'MARTHA ISAACSON', and the azalea hybrid 'IRENE KOSTER'. The following are other North American azalea species:

VISCOSUM, (USDA 5) 'The Swamp Honeysuckle', is useful for its tolerance of sites wetter than those normally suitable for rhododendrons. Similar to *occidentale*, with white and pink, rather smaller, scented flowers. July.

PRINOPHYLLUM has pink, scented flowers in May. Very hardy.

VASEYI is a distinct, hardy species with pink flowers, often spotted green. 'White Find' is a fine white form. Superb autumn colour.

CALENDULACEUM, in contrast to the above, has striking orange flowers or occasionally red or yellow.

CANADENSE (USDA 5) is an early-flowered species with mauve or white flowers on the bare stems in April–May. Very hardy, suitable for any UK garden. Low-growing and good in moist sites.

occidentale

SCHLIPPENBACHII

H4 low-medium May 6b–5/6a

One of the finest of all deciduous species, with large pink (occasionally white) flowers in good trusses. Larger leaves than other azalea species, on a plant compact and well-shaped in full sun, but which gets leggy in shade. The growth comes rather early and can be damaged severely by late frosts. Very hardy, but the early new growth makes it unsuitable for gardens much colder than Glendoick. Hard to root, and so either grafted on LUTEUM (beware of suckers) or from hand-pollinated seed, but only the best forms should be used as parents or rather average seedlings can be produced. Now some clones are in tissue culture. **'Prince Charming'** F.C.C. is a fine clone, but it is rarely available.

ALBRECHTII has smaller showy flowers, best in its bright rose-purple forms; Paler rose forms also exist. Like *schlippenbachii*, it is early into growth.

HYBRIDS

Available in colours ranging from white, yellow, pink, orange and red, and in many combinations of these colours, they are best planted in mixed groups. For massed planting, it is cheapest to buy seedling hybrids which are usually available by colour. There are also hundreds of named clones derived originally from several large breeding programs which have given their names to some of the categories of hybrids e.g. 'Knap Hill' and 'Ghent'. The hybrids are sun- and semi-shade-tolerant, very hardy, easy plants, reaching an ultimate size of up to 6ft × 6ft (1.8m × 1.8m) or more in favourable conditions. They flower in May and June, and many are scented.

GHENT HYBRIDS are the oldest of the deciduous azalea hybrids, derived from crossing the European species *luteum* with North American species such as *calendulaceum* and *viscosum*. These and the 'Rustica Flore Pleno' hybrids are back in fashion, as they tend to be of pastel colours, more subtle than the bright Exbury hybrids. Taller-growing than Mollis. Good autumn colour. Some are scented.

RUSTICA FLORE PLENO. A series of pastel-coloured, small double-flowered hybrids which have been almost lost from commerce, but are seeing revived interest.

MOLLIS. Bred mainly in Europe in the 19th century from the Japanese species *japonicum* and little different from selections of this species. These are the earliest-flowering azalea group, opening in the first half of May in most places. Shades of red, orange and pink. Seldom more than 5ft (1.5m) in height, so good for smaller gardens.

KNAP HILL. Original clones were bred at the Knaphill nursery in Surrey by combining the Ghent and Mollis strains, and these hybrids were then used for further breeding at Exbury, Windsor and several other places in other parts of the world. The Chinese species *molle* was used in the breeding at Exbury. There are now hundreds of named clones. This is the brightest-coloured and most popular of the azalea hybrids. The best clones have large full trusses of five-lobed flowers of white, yellow, orange and red, and some are a combination of two or more colours. Some are scented.

OCCIDENTALE. Raised from the American species (q.v.), these have paler flowers than the Exbury and Knaphills but are more strongly scented in most clones and usually later-flowering.

'LIGHTS'. A new group of very hardy azaleas bred in Minnesota, USA. Freely produced small flowers. The clones available so far are 'ORCHID LIGHTS'—purplish pink, 'ROSY LIGHTS' rose, 'WHITE LIGHTS' white and yellow; scented. Other clones are being released and will soon be available.

Clones

There are so many named clones that it is only possible to mention those most commonly commercially available. Most named deciduous azalea hybrids are perfectly good, varying little in hardiness, and ease of cultivation. All begin flowering from mid to late May, unless stated otherwise.

BERRYROSE (Knaphill) Salmon-pink flowers, red on the tube, with a yellow flare open in late May. Coppery young growth. A.M. 1934. One of the best in this colour.

BRAZIL (Knaphill) Bright tangerine orange and red, deepening the longer the flowers are out, with frilled edges to the petals.

CECILE (Knaphill) Deep buds open to large salmon-pink flowers with a yellow flare. We do not find this very vigorous.

COCCINEA SPECIOSA (Ghent) Small tangerine-red and yellow flowers in rounded trusses giving an effect like deep honeysuckle. An old hybrid which is very free-flowering, and still well worth growing. Late May.

DAVIESII (Ghent) One of the best of the Ghents, with a subtle combination of pale yellow, pink and white, with a deeper yellow blotch. Sweetly scented. Quite low-growing, with a suckering habit. Late May/early June. There are two clones, the UK one with double flowers, the USA one with more ordinary single ones.

DR M. OOSTHOEK (Mollis) Deep orange-red with a deeper flare in the throat. One of the best deep-coloured Mollis clones. Late May. A.M.T. 1940.

FIREBALL (Knaphill) Deep orange-red flowers in full trusses with contrasting yellow stamens. Coppery to deep-red new growth.

'Homebush A.M.T. & Hotspur' A.M.

GEORGE REYNOLDS (Knaphill) One of the parents of many of the Exbury hybrids. Large deep-yellow flowers, slightly marked green, with deeper yellow/orange spotting in the throat. Tall growing. A.M. 1936.

GIBRALTAR (Knaphill) The most popular and widely available azalea hybrid in the UK. Deep orange-red flowers, serrated and frilled at the edges, yellow in the throat, in a large full truss.

GLOWING EMBERS (Knaphill) Orange-red with an orange flare. Compact habit.

GOLDEN SUNSET (Knaphill) Orange-red buds open to light-yellow flowers, tinged orange, and with an orange flare in the throat. A.M. 1956.

HOMEBUSH (Knaphill-Ghent type) Ball-shaped trusses of semi-double deep carmine-pink flowers, giving a pompon effect. Unusual, and the most widely available azalea of this type. A.M.T. 1950.

'Hotspur' A.M.

'Irene Koster'

HOTSPUR (Knaphill) Orange-red flowers with a yellow flare. 'Hotspur Red' was originally a different clone, but now the two names are probably synonymous. A.M. 1934.

IRENE KOSTER (Occidentale) White flushed crimson and pink, with a yellow flare in the throat. Very fine scent. June.

KATHLEEN (Knaphill) Deep pink buds open salmon-pink, with an orange blotch. Similar to 'CECILE' but with more orange in the flower.

KLONDYKE (Knaphill) Reddish orange buds open to deep golden-yellow flowers, salmon-red on the backs of the petals. One of the best yellows. Coppery red new growth.

'Klondyke' ►

'Strawberry Ice' A.M.T.

KOSTER'S BRILLIANT RED (Mollis) There are probably several different clones of this in the trade. Orange-red flowers.

NARCISSIFLORA syn 'Narcissiflorum' (Ghent) Double pale-yellow flowers, deeper in the centre and on outsides of the petals. Sweetly scented. Vigorous, and upright growing. Bronzy autumn colour. F.C.C.T. 1923.

PERSIL (Knaphill) One of the most striking of the white-flowered Knaphill hybrids, but due to rooting difficulties, it has been rather scarce. Now produced by micro-propagation, it should become more widely available. Large pure white flowers with a deep yellow flare in the throat. '**Oxydol**' is quite similar.

ROYAL COMMAND (Knaphill) Vivid reddish-orange flowers which fade to yellow in full sun. Good autumn colour.

SATAN (Knaphill) Deep red buds open geranium red. One of the nearest to true reds.

SILVER SLIPPER (Knaphill) Creamy white with a yellow flare, and pink tinges. Reddish-bronze new growth. Fragrant. June. F.C.C.T. 1963.

SPEK'S ORANGE (Mollis) Bright orange flowers, deeper in the throat, with green markings. Later than most Mollis clones, flowering in the second half of May. F.C.C.T. 1953.

STRAWBERRY ICE (Knaphill) Flesh pink, flushed deeper pink, with a yellow throat. Large full trusses, and an unusual colour combination. A.M.T. 1962.

TUNIS (Knaphill) Deep crimson with an orange throat.

WHITE LIGHTS ('Lights') Small white flowers with golden markings. Scented. One of a new race of very hardy Canadian hybrids. Pink and lavender clones also exist.

EVERGREEN OR JAPANESE AZALEAS

This well known group of plants is now classified as a subgroup of Rhododendron. The Japanese or evergreen azaleas are hardy relations of the well-known 'indica' azalea commonly grown as a houseplant, and indeed the two are similar in appearance. They vary in height from a few inches to over 6ft (1.8m) and are available in a range of colours from white through pink, red and orange-red to purple. They are best planted in clumps or beds on their own, rather than with dwarf rhododendrons or other plants. Carefully chosen, there are plenty of varieties suitable for almost any UK climate, but undoubtedly they are most successful in warmer, sunnier areas.

In the south, the best displays, such as the bowl in Windsor Great Park Valley Gardens, are seen in light woodland. In the north, where the sun is less strong, they need to be planted in the open to flower well and to ensure that their wood is sufficiently ripened to withstand the winter. Many of the varieties most commonly sold in the UK may be suitable for the south of England but are certainly far from ideal further north. Over the years new varieties have been imported from the USA, Canada, Holland and Germany and we have bred some of our own hybrids. Such varieties are mentioned in the descriptions as being particularly successful in colder and more northern gardens. In the west, where rainfall is high, evergreen azaleas often grow into rather straggly plants, while in the east they tend to remain more compact. They like a well-drained soil, and even quite dry conditions, and provide a spectacular display in May and early June. Those described as 'early' start flowering in early to mid-May in the south and west, mid-May further north. 'Late' generally means flowering from early June onwards.

There are over 200 different evergreen azalea hybrids currently commercially available in the UK. The following is a selection of the most widely grown older varieties, and our selection of the best of the new ones:

'**ADDY WERY**' One of the most popular, and widely available. An early-flowering tall, upright grower with bright bronzy scarlet or vermilion flowers. A.M.T. 1950.

'**ADVANCE**' Vivid reddish-purple flowers on a dense medium-sized plant with pale green leaves, flowering mid-season. Quite widely available.

'**AMOENUM**' (syn. Amoena) One of the first azaleas to be introduced from Shanghai, China by R. Fortune in 1850. A low spreader with hose-in-hose rosy purple flowers. '**Amoenum Coccineum**' is a sport of the above with carmine-rose flowers. Rather unstable and inclined to revert. Not for coldest areas.

'Diamant Rosy Red'

'BEETHOVEN' Large lilac-mauve flowers, nearly 3in (8cm) in diameter, with deeper spotting in the centre. One of the most popular of the purple azaleas.

'BLAAW'S PINK' Hose-in-hose flowers, salmon-pink, deeper at the edge, paler in the centre and slightly spotted. Early. Widely available.

'BLUE DANUBE' One of the most striking in this shade. Relatively large bluish-violet flowers on a low compact dense bush. Fairly early. Unfortunately, not reliably hardy in Scotland, but excellent further south. F.C.C.T. 1975.

'CHIPPEWA' A fine new azalea from the USA; bright-pink flowers on a low spreading plant. Late.

'DIAMANT' (syn. Diamond) A group of extremely hardy azaleas which we introduced from Europe. Amongst the most successful of all for Scotland and Northern England. The colours available are 'Lilac', 'Pink', 'Rosy Red', 'Salmon Pink' and 'White'. All are very compact, low-growing and free-flowering.

'ELIZABETH GABLE' Large deep-red, frilled flowers, deeper in the throat. Late. Spreading habit. Not very good in Scotland.

'FAVORITE' An old Dutch hybrid, still widely available. Vivid deep-rosy-pink flowers on a dense, free-flowering bush with glossy leaves. Early.

'HATSUGURI' An early-flowering, low spreader with magenta flowers. We find that it looks rather scruffy by the spring. F.C.C.T. 1967.

'HINO CRIMSON' A fairly low-growing bright crimson which holds its colour well. Good foliage, reddish in winter. Not hardy in Eastern Scotland, suffering bark-split. H.C.T. 1974.

'HINODEGIRI' One of the first azaleas to be introduced from Japan during the 19th century. Bright red, deeper in the throat. A medium compact, early flowerer. A.M.T. 1965.

'HINOMAYO' Another of the earliest azaleas to be introduced, and still very widely grown. Small but very bright phlox-pink flowers on a compact dense grower. Loses most of its leaves in winter, especially in colder areas. F.C.C.T. 1945.

'JOHANNA' Carmine-red flowers. One of the best azaleas for foliage, which is dark and shiny, and the plant looks good all the year round. A.M. 1988.

'JOHN CAIRNS' Quite large indian red, or brownish-scarlet flowers, spotted deeper. Quite tall-growing, but densely clad, with small leaves which turn reddish and bronzy in winter. A.M.T. 1940.

'KERMESINA' An excellent very hardy Dutch hybrid, ideal for Scotland. Bright pink flowers on a very compact plant with shiny leaves. A sport of the above has been recently introduced from West Germany, **'KERMESINA ROSE'**, which has unusual pink and white flowers. The flowers tend to revert sporadically, but this is one of the most striking azaleas we have seen, and it is bound to become very popular.

'Kermesina Rose'

'Orange Beauty' F.C.C.T.

'KIRIN' A Kurume with flowers of two shades of pink hose-in-hose and a coloured calyx. Not very hardy, only suitable for south and west. A.M.T. 1961.

KIUSIANUM This Japanese species is a parent of many of the most popular azalea hybrids, and is well worth growing in its own right. Very hardy, free-flowering and good in Scotland, it is largely deciduous, and in most forms, has a very low, compact habit with tiny leaves. Many different coloured forms exist, including white, pink, purplish-pink, rose-red, and orange-red.

'LEMUR' One of our own hybrids, raised from the dwarf Japanese species ***NAKAHARAE***. Deep pink long-lasting flowers, and shiny leaves. A low compact spreader. Becoming quite widely available. H.C.T. 1988.

◄ 'Mucronatum' A.M.

'LEO' An Exbury hybrid with large salmon-orange flowers late in the season, on a low, spreading bush.

'MOTHER'S DAY' Large crimson flowers, sometimes semi-double. Fairly large, glossy, darkish green leaves, bronzy in winter, on a low spreading plant. Late. One of the most popular, and very widely available. Unfortunately very susceptible to azalea gall fungus. F.C.C.T. 1970.

'MUCRONATUM' (syn. 'Ledifolia Alba') Introduced from Japan in 1819, this is one of the oldest of all cultivated azaleas. Large white flowers on an upright plant, with distinctive pointed hairy leaves. One of the best white-flowered azaleas for Scotland, and quite widely available. A.M. 1921.

'Panda'

NAKAHARAE An excellent reasonably hardy Taiwanese species which flowers later than most other evergreen azaleas, sometimes into August. We recommend two clones: '**Mariko**' A.M. 1980—relatively large salmon red flowers, on one of the most dwarf of all evergreen azaleas: it forms tight impenetrable mounds a few inches high, with tiny deep green leaves, '**Mt Seven Star**' has larger leaves on a creeping plant with bright red flowers. Both are hardy in Scotland.

'ORANGE BEAUTY' One of the most popular salmon-orange-flowered azaleas, on a fairly low-growing compact plant. Best in some shade in the south to preserve the flower colour. Quite satisfactory in Scotland. Early. F.C.C.T. 1958.

'PALESTRINA' Once the standard white azalea, this has now been superseded, but is still commercially available. Large white flowers, with greenish markings in the throat. An erect narrow grower which can get rather sparse. Said to be more than one clone in existence; the one we had was useless in our climate. F.C.C. 1967.

'PANDA' One of our own introductions, this is destined to become one of the most popular of all white evergreen azaleas. Pure white flowers on a compact grower with light green leaves. Hardy and very successful in Scotland.

'PURPLE TRIUMPH' Fairly large deep-purple flowers on a spreading bush. Mid-season. Raised in Holland. A.M.T. 1960.

'ROSEBUD' Unusual rose-pink flowers like minature rose buds. A very compact upright grower which flowers later than most. Not the hardiest azalea, but damaged only in the severest winters at Glendoick. Not recommended for coldest areas. A.M.T. 1972.

'SQUIRREL' Another of our own introductions. Long-lasting bright scarlet flowers on a medium grower with fine foliage. Fairly late. Very good in Scotland.

'STEWARTSTONIAN' (syn. Stewartsoniana) Deep brownish-red flowers, glossy leaves, bronzy in winter. Similar to 'Addy Wery'.

'VELVET GOWN' Raised by the firm of Waterer, this is a low spreading plant with dark-green leaves and rich-purple flowers. Late.

'VIDA BROWN' A very compact, low-growing plant with tiny leaves. Late, large, hose-in-hose, deep-pink flowers. Very slow-growing. A.M.T. 1960.

'VUYK'S ROSY RED' A popular Dutch hybrid with large rosy-red flowers, and glossy foliage. A medium grower, which flowers in late May and early June. Not completely hardy in Scotland, occasionally suffering bark-split. F.C.C.T. 1988.

'VUYK'S SCARLET' Probably the most popular of all evergreen azaleas in the UK. Fine crimson flowers, and glossy foliage. F.C.C.T. 1966. A good performer in Scotland, and very widely commercially available.

'WILLY' Large clear rosy-pink flowers on a medium-sized bush with semi-deciduous leaves which turn bronzy or red before falling. Mid-season. The best of the Dutch *kaempferi* hybrids for colder and more northern gardens.

'Squirrel'

'WOMBAT' One of our own introductions. A vigorous low-growing carpeter which opens its bright pink flowers in late May and early June. Very good in Scotland.

LISTS

These lists are intended to assist in choosing rhododendrons for specific purposes, and include a few choices of a necessarily subjective nature. Many of the lists could easily be longer than they are, so an omission does not deny suitability. Often a species or hybrid has many near relatives which could equally well be included. In some cases only the best clones of a species will satisfy the given characteristic. This is particularly true of glaucous foliage.

Easy species for the small garden
dichroanthum, fastigiatum/impeditum, ferrugineum, hippophaeoides, keleticum, mekongense Viridescens, *yakushimanum*.

Easy species for the larger garden
arboreum, bureavii, campylocarpum, decorum, oreodoxa, rex ssp. *fictolacteum, rubiginosum, wardii, yunnanense*.

Early flowering
(*a*) relatively frost-hardy flowers: *dauricum, lapponicum, moupinense, mucronulatum, oreodoxa*, hybrids of these, 'Christmas Cheer'.
(*b*) more frost-tender flowers: *barbatum, calophytum, strigillosum*, 'Bo Peep', 'Cilpinense', 'Nobleanum', 'Seta', 'Snow Lady', 'Tessa'.

Late flowering
auriculatum, facetum, griersonianum, hemsleyanum, heliolepis, occidentale, sanguineum ssp. *didymum, viscosum*, 'Azor', 'Polar Bear', 'Lodauric' etc.

Best foliage
(*a*) indumentum: *bureavii, falconeri/eximeum, haematodes, mallotum, pachysanthum, tsariense, yakushimanum*/'Ken Janek' and many hybrids of these and other species.
(*b*) glaucous leaves (many of these species are variable, not all forms showing glaucous leaves, so seek out the best): *campanulatum* ssp. *aeruginosum, campylocarpum* ssp. *caloxanthum, cinnabarinum, fastigiatum, lepidostylum, oreotrephes, mekongense* Viridescens, *thomsonii*, 'Intrifast'.
(*c*) overall foliage effect: *insigne* (metallic leaf under-surface), *lutescens* (red foliage), *orbiculare/williamsianum* (round leaves), *roxieanum* var. *oreonastes*, (spiky effect of leaves), *sinogrande* (largest leaves), and many others.

Drier sites
decorum, macrophyllum, moupinense, racemosum, rubiginosum, the Triflora SS and hybrids of the above species.

Severest gardens and coldest sites
dauricum, catawbiense, hippophaeoides, mucronulatum, smirnowii, yakushimanum, 'Arctic Tern', 'Ramapo', 'P.J.M.', and hundreds of hardy hybrids such as 'Gomer Waterer', 'Nova Zembla', 'Scarlet Wonder' etc., hardier 'yak' hybrids, e.g. 'Bashful', 'Morgenrot'.

Milder coastal gardens in south and west
arboreum, edgeworthii, facetum, falconeri, griffithianum, lindleyi, macabeanum, sinogrande, valentinianum, 'Harry Tagg', 'Lady Alice Fitzwilliam' and similar hybrids.

Best white flowers
dauricum Hokkaido, *decorum, lindleyi, rex* ssp. *fictolacteum, rigidum, yakushimanum*, 'Arctic Tern', 'Dora Amateis', 'Helene Schiffner', 'Loderi King George', 'Ptarmigan'.

Best pink flowers
oreodoxa, racemosum, souliei (pink forms), *williamsianum, yunnannense* (pink forms), 'Anna Baldsiefen', 'Christmas Cheer', 'Fantastica', 'Scintillation', *williamsianum*

hybrids e.g. 'Linda', 'Pink Pebble', 'Whisperingrose'.

Best yellow flowers
campylocarpum, keiskei, macabeanum, valentinianum, wardii, 'Crest', 'Curlew', 'Hotei', 'Odee Wright', 'Yellowhammer'.

Best red flowers
barbatum, forrestii Repens R. 59174, *griersonianum, haematodes, strigillosum, thomsonii*, 'David', 'Dopey', 'Grace Seabrook', 'Jean Marie de Montague', 'Markeeta's Prize', 'Vulcan'.

Best purple/blue flowers
augustinii, fastigiatum, keleticum, niveum, russatum, 'Azurwolke', 'Blue Peter', 'Purple Splendour', 'St Merryn', 'Susan'.

Best orange flowers
cinnabarinum Concatenans, *citriniflorum* ssp. *horaeum* F. 21850, *dichroanthum, viscidifolium*, 'Fabia', 'Goldsworth Orange', 'Medusa', 'September Song', 'Sonata', 'Trewithen Orange', 'Viscy'.

Best multi-coloured/changing-coloured flowers
'Cinnkeys', 'Lampion', 'Lem's Cameo', 'Riplet', 'Virginia Richards', 'Vanessa Pastel'.

Scent
(*a*) hardier: *auriculatum, decorum, fortunei, luteum, occidentale, viscosum*, Loderi, 'Martha Isaacson', 'Mrs A.T. de La Mare', 'Polar Bear', 'Lodauric' and similar hybrids.
(*b*) more tender: *edgeworthii, formosum* ssp. *inaequale, griffithianum, lindleyi, maddenii*, 'Fragrantissimum', 'Lady Alice Fitzwilliam', etc.

Neutral or slightly alkaline soil
augustinii, ciliatum, decorum, hirsutum, rubiginosum, sanguineum ssp. *didymum, vernicosum*, 'Cunningham's White' (and plants grafted onto it), 'Emasculum'.

Favourite smaller hybrids
'Arctic Tern', 'Curlew', 'Egret', 'Ginny Gee', 'Goldilocks', 'Merganser', 'Razorbill', 'Riplet', 'St Merryn', 'Too Bee and Not Too Bee' ('Wee Bee').

Favourite 'Yak' hybrids
'Dopey', 'Fantastica', 'Hydon Dawn', 'Ken Janeck', 'Lampion', 'Percy Wiseman', 'Seven Stars', 'Titian Beauty'.

Favourite larger hybrids
'Crest', 'Golden Star', 'Grace Seabrook'/'Taurus', 'Lem's Cameo', 'Lem's Monarch', 'Odee Wright', 'Sir Charles Lemon', 'Vanessa Pastel', 'Virginia Richards'.

Best evergreen azaleas
'Johanna', *kiusianum*, 'Kermesina', 'Kirin' (tender), 'Mucronatum', 'Panda', 'Vuyk's Scarlet'.

Curiosities
'Arctic Tern', (bi-generic hybrid?), 'Creamy Chiffon' (double flowers), 'Elizabeth Lockhart' (purple leaves), 'Goldflimmer'/'President Roosevelt'/'Ponticum Variegatum' (variegated leaves), 'Martha Isaacson' (azaleodendron).

Best newer introductions
(*a*) species: *hemsleyanum, keiskei* 'Yaku Fairy', *kesangiae*.
(*b*) hybrids: 'Azurwolke', 'Brigitte', 'Fantastica', 'Lampion', 'Too Bee/Not Too Bee' ('Wee Bee'), 'Nancy Evans', 'Rubicon', 'Sacko', *pachysanthum*.

Species, a connoisseur's choice
Some are quite hard to please, but are well worth extra care.
(*a*) smaller: *calostrotum* Gigha, *camtschaticum, campylogynum, citriniflorum* ssp. *horaeum* F. 21850, *forrestii* var. Repens R. 59174, *megeratum, proteoides, recurvoides, sargentianum, tsariense*.
(*b*) medium: *haematodes, insigne, lacteum, pachysanthum, pseudochrysanthum, roxieanum, schlippenbachii, souliei, wardii* L&S.
(*c*) larger: *falconeri, griffithianum, lanigerum, lindleyi, niveum, sinogrande, montroseanum*.

A NOTE ON CLASSIFICATION

We have followed the Edinburgh revisions in the classification of rhododendron species. People have objected to the very long names which the new revisions have produced. While this is necessary for correct botanical discussion, it is in no way essential for general horticulture and so we have shortened names thus: *campylocarpum* ssp. *campylocarpum* becomes *campylocarpum*. We retain the two names when the species and the subspecies epithets are different. e.g.*campylocarpum* ssp. *caloxanthum*. This makes the name much easier, and we hope that this will become the norm for publications of a non-botanical nature.

GLOSSARY

AZALEA GALL A fungal disease which produces ugly distortions on evergreen azaleas and a few rhododendrons. Best picked off by hand, and there are fungicides available to help control it.

BARK-SPLIT Caused by early or late frosts while the plant is growing, freezing the sap in the stems and splitting the bark. This can happen to plants which are otherwise perfectly hardy. It can be fatal on small plants. Early growth is worth protecting in frosty weather.

CALYX The outermost part of a flower, where it joins on to the stalk which holds it. Some calyces are large and coloured, giving a double effect.

CHLOROSIS The yellowing of leaves, due to mineral deficiency, water (too little or too much), climatic or genetic problems.

CLONE A (named) clone is one propagated asexually by cuttings, tissue-culture, grafts or layers, and is genetically identical to the parent plant. See also 'grex'.

ELEPIDOTE One of two main groups into which rhododendrons are classified. The chief characteristic is the lack of scales on the leaf. This group includes most of the larger-growing species, and they cannot be hybridized with the other group—the lepidotes (q.v.).

GLAUCOUS Refers to leaves which have a waxy sheen, usually blue-green or grey-green. Glaucous foliage is generally considered attractive in rhododendrons.

GREX The seedlings of a hybrid cross are called a grex. At one time all the seedlings, good and bad, were allowed to take the hybrid name, e.g. 'Fabia' but now each seedling must have its own clonal name (see clone). Hybrids originally released as a grex (g.) are mentioned in the text.

HOSE-IN-HOSE Applied to a flower with two rims of petals, giving a double effect. Most common in evergreen azaleas.

INDUMENTUM A woolly or hairy covering on the leaf or stem. This is generally a prized characteristic, found most often on species rather than hybrids, which adds to the year-round attraction of a bush.

LEPIDOTE One of two main groups into which rhododendrons are classified. The main characteristic is the scales on the leaves. This group contains most of the smaller species, and these cannot be hybridized with the other group, the elepidotes (q.v.).

POWDERY MILDEW A fungal disease which has recently appeared, and which is undoubtedly the worst disease to afflict rhododendrons. Brown or grey patches appear on the lower leaf surface, with yellow mottling on the upper surface. Bad attacks cause defoliation and can kill the plant. As yet only preventative fungicides exist, which should be sprayed on susceptible plants from May to September. Certain groups of rhododendron are particularly susceptible, and these are noted in the text. Best prevented by planting in open sites where there is free movement of air.

RUST A less serious fungal disease than

the above, it attacks mainly hybrid rhododendrons. Effectively controlled by spraying. It is identified by powdery orange patches on the leaf underside.

SS Subsection. Related rhododendron species are classified into groups called subsections.

TRUSS A group of flowers which join one rhachis or flower-stalk. Rhododendrons have trusses of 2–40+ flowers, depending on the variety, the trusses varying greatly in shape from upright to loose.

TUBE The part of the flower at the base, surrounding the stigma and stamens, often tubular in shape.

FURTHER INFORMATION

Literature available on rhododendrons is extensive. The following is a selection of the most widely available books and journals. In addition to these, there are books on the subject produced in many other parts of the world, including several well-illustrated ones produced in China.

BOOKS

SPECIES AND HYBRIDS: W. J. Bean, *Trees and Shrubs Hardy in the British Isles*, Vol. III, 8th Revised Edition; P. A. Cox, *The Smaller Rhododendrons*; K. N. E. Cox, *Rhododendrons, A Plantsman's Guide*; D. G. Leach, *Rhododendrons of the World*; Royal Horticultural Society, *Rhododendron Year Book* 1946–71, *Rhododendrons*, 1972–3, *Rhododendrons with Magnolias and Camellias*, 1974 onwards; American Rhododendron Society, *Quarterly Bulletin*, 1947–81, *Journal*, 1982 onwards.

SPECIES: P. A. Cox, *The Larger Species of Rhododendron*; H. H. Davidian, *The Rhododendron Species Vol. I Lepidotes*, and *Vol. II Elepidotes*; Royal Horticultural Society, *The Rhododendron Handbook*, *Rhododendron Species in Cultivation*, 1980.

HYBRIDS: P. A. & K. N. E. Cox, *Encyclopedia of Rhododendron Hybrids*; H. E. Salley & H. E. Greer, *Rhododendron Hybrids, A Guide to Their Origins*; J. F. Street, *Hardy Rhododendrons* and *Rhododendrons*; C. Fairweather, *Rhododendrons and Azaleas*; C. E. Phillips & P. N. Barker, *The Rothschild Rhododendrons*.

AZALEAS: F. C. Galle, *Azaleas*; F. P. Lee, *The Azalea Book*; J. F. Street, *Azaleas*.

RHODODENDRON SOCIETIES

The best advice to a new enthusiast would be to join one of the Rhododendron societies which hold shows, meetings, lectures, and garden tours, and produce journals and newsletters.

Great Britain

The Rhododendron and Camellia Group, c/o The Royal Horticultural Society, P.O. Box 313, Vincent Square, London SW1P 2PE. Regional meetings also take place.

The Scottish Rhododendron Society (Scottish Chapter of the American Rhododendron Society), Hubert Andrew, Stron Ailne, Colintrave, Argyll PA22 3AS.

EUROPE

DENMARK: The Danish Chapter of the American Rhododendron Society, Ole. Packendah, Hejrebakken 3, DK 3500 Vaerloese.

WEST GERMANY: German Rhododendron Society, Dr L. Heft, Rhododendron Park, 28 Bremen 17, Marcusalle 60.

SWEDEN: The Swedish Rhododendron Society, Botaniska Trädgården, Carl Skothsbergs Gata 22, Goteborg.

U.S.A.

The American Rhododendron Society, Executive Secretary, 14885 S.W. Sunrise Lane, Tigard, OR 97224.

Pacific Rhododendron Society, PO Box 297, Puyallup, WA 98371.

The Rhododendron Species Foundation, PO Box 3798, Federal Way, WA 98063.

CANADA
Rhododendron Society of Canada, Dr H. G. Hedges, 4271 Lakeshore Rd., Burlington, Ont.

AUSTRALIA
Australian Rhododendron Society, Mrs L. Eaton, PO Box 21, Olinda, Victoria, 3788.

NEW ZEALAND
New Zealand Rhododendron Association, PO Box 28, Palmerston North.

Dunedin Rhododendron Group, S. J. Grant, 25 Pollack St., Dunedin.

WHERE TO OBTAIN RHODODENDRONS

If you can't find what you want in your local garden centre, there are several excellent specialist nurseries in Britain which offer a mail-order service. Some export. All have a catalogue which can be obtained for a small charge. Most are also open for personal callers. The size of plant offered and the prices charged vary enormously, so shop around!

GREAT BRITAIN

Glendoick Gardens Ltd, Perth PH2 7NS, Scotland. Our own nursery which specializes in dwarf rhododendrons, species, (esp. from wild seed) and new hybrid introductions from around the world. We export. Also Garden Centre.
Hydon Nurseries, Clock Barn Lane, Hydon Heath, Godalming, Surrey. Famous for their Chelsea displays.
Leonardslee Garden Nurseries, Woodreeves, Mill Lane, Lower Bleeding, Horsham, West Sussex RH13 6PX. Specializes in grafts of species and hybrids.
Millais Nurseries, Crosswater Farm, Churt, Farnham, Surrey GU10 2JN. A small nursery with a wide range of species and older and newer hybrids.
G. Reuthe Ltd. Crown Pt. Nursery, Sevenoaks Rd., Ightham, rn. Sevenoaks, Kent.
Starborough Nursery, Starborough Road, Marsh Green, Edenbridge, Kent TN8 5RB.
Wall Cottage Nursery, Lockengate, Bugle, St. Austell, Cornwall. Specialities include species and hybrids propagated from Cornish gardens.

EUROPE
Firma C. Esveld, Rijneveld 72, 2771 XS, Boskoop, Holland.
Joh Wieting, Omorikastrase 6, 1910 Gieselhorst, Westerstede 1, West Germany.
Pieter Zwijnenburg Jr., Halve Raak 18, 2771 AD Boskoop, Holland.

USA
Benjamin's Rhododendrons, PO Box 147, Sumner, WA 98390
Briarwood Gardens, 14 Gully Lane, RFD 1, East Sandwich, MA 02537
Eastern Plant Specialities, PO Box 226, Georgetown, Maine 04548
Ellanhurst Gardens, Rt. 3, Box 233–B, Sherwood, OR 97140
Greer Gardens, 1280 Goodpasture Island Rd, Eugene, OR 97401–1794
Hall Rhododendrons, PO Box 62, Drain, OR 97435
Homeplace Garden, PO Box 300, Commerce, GA 30529
Hammond's Acres of Rhododendrons, 25911– 70th Ave. N.E., Arlington, WA 98223
Mowbray Gardens, 3318 Mowbray Lane, Cincinnati, OH 45226
North Coast Rhododendron Nursery, PO Box 308, Bodega, CA 94922
Rhododendron Species Foundation, Box 3798, Federal Way, WA 98063
Roslyn Nursery, Dept A, PO Box 69, Roslyn, NY 11576
Sonoma Horticultural Nursery, 3970 Azalea Ave., Sebastopol, CA 95472
The Bovees Nursery, 1737 S.W. Coronado, Portland, OR 97219
The Greenery, 14450 N.E. 16th Place, Bellevue, WA 98007
Transplant Nursery, Parkertown Rd., Lavonia, GA 30553
Westgate Gardens Nursery, 751 Westgate Drive, Eureka, CA
Weston Nurseries, Hopkinton, WA 01748
Whitney Gardens and Nursery, PO Box F, Brinnon, WA 98320

AUSTRALIA

Cedar Lodge Nursery, Creamery Rd., Sulphur Creek, Tasmania 7321

P. & C. Deen Sons, Monbulk Rd., Kallista, 3791, Victoria

Lapoinya Rhododendron Gardens, R.S.D. 106A, Lapoinya, Tasmania, 7325

Woodbank Nursery, R.M.B. 303, Kingston, Tasmania 7150

NEW ZEALAND

Cross Hills Gardens, R.D. 54, Kimbolton

Riverwood Gardens, Main Rd., Little River, Banks Peninsular

INDEX

Figures in italics indicate main text entries; figures in bold indicate photographs.